W9-CBN-735

PETER KREEFT
THE SNAKEBITE LETTERS

PETER KREEFT

THE SNAKEBITE LETTERS

Devilishly Devious Secrets for
Subverting Society
As Taught in Tempter's Training School

IGNATIUS PRESS   SAN FRANCISCO

Originally published in
The National Catholic Register
© 1991 Twin Circle Publishing Company

Cover design by Roxanne Mei Lum

Published 1993 Ignatius Press, San Francisco
ISBN 0-89870-449-9
Library of Congress catalogue number 93-77208
Printed in the United States of America

CONTENTS

INTRODUCTION

Reader: Humph! This book sounds suspiciously like a shameless plagiarism of C. S. Lewis' *Screwtape Letters.*

Author: It is! I have no shame about it, because I'm sure Lewis *wanted* such "plagiarisms". *The Screwtape Letters* invented a new genre, a new *species;* all I'm doing is breeding another *specimen.*

Humph anyway! Letters from a devil, isn't it?

Yep. And I ain't telling where I got 'em.

But devils and demons and evil spirits—are you trying to restore the Inquisition?

No, but it sounds as if *you* are.

But the very idea is so—so *negative!*

Yes. Evil is rather negative, I think.

You're one of those neo-nazi, fascist, racist, sexist, homophobic, white, American males, aren't you? Why, I'll bet you're even (spit! choke!) *religious.*

Oh, worse than that. Christian. Catholic, even.

You people are all so hopelessly . . . (*searching for the ultimate put-down*) . . . *conservative!*

Politically incorrect, you mean? Oh, happily and wholeheartedly so.

Well, I certainly won't waste *my* time reading such closedminded, negativistic, prejudiced, name-calling, venomous nonsense!

Yes, I can see that. Say, are there any mirrors in your house?

What?

When you stand in front of one, do you see any reflection?

I don't need this kind of abuse. I'm leaving.

Good-bye. And congratulations.

Congratulations? For what?

For knowing what I've written before you've read it. It's rare to meet such divine foreknowledge.

That's what I mean—nasty. You're demonizing your opponents.

No, just the opposite. I just divinized you. Don't you know the difference? Is *that* the definition of a liberal?

See? You're demonizing us!

No, laughing at you. This book is satire. It's you people who never seem to laugh, only sneer. Now, please stop sputtering and get out of my book. I have more important fish to fry.

I

ON SPIRITUAL WARFARE

My dear nephew Braintwister:

As your great-uncle I was, of course, signally pleased when the Education Directorate asked me to train you as the new case officer for Patient No. 66,589/ADFgm. As a veteran, I do so enjoy working with fresh talent from the academy.

It's an unusual honor to be assigned to a new patient in the middle of his life. So perhaps you've been "noticed" by the Lower Downs. Doubtless you've also been briefed on the terrain: the regrettable failure of Wormhole, the comrade you're replacing, and the patient's recent conversion to the Enemy's Church. However, as I shall demonstrate below, all is not lost—by any means.

Take a lesson from Wormhole, though. Hell, unlike the Opposition, focuses quite realistically on results. Remember the ruling slogan of your plebe-year philosophy seminar: "Nothing succeeds but success." I also encourage you to review the fine print of your executive-incentive plan.

I'll miss Wormhole, naturally, but his work had been shoddy since the Cure d'Ars fiasco. And it's only fitting that the final act of his long, if undistinguished, career should be to nourish and refresh his fellow officers. I must say it's a gourmet's delight when a former comrade is sauteed to perfection for the rest of us to savor. The quality of human souls is so decidedly bland lately.

Well, to the business at hand: Your patient has become a

Catholic. A modest setback. You novices don't realize how even an inconvenience like this can be turned to our advantage. This may shock you, since the Church is our only remaining earthly enemy of any substance, and his conversion to that Church is sincere—for the moment. But you forget that your patient is American; delightfully, typically American.

What does that mean? A Catholic college professor recently polled his students and found that the vast majority of them, by their own reckoning, thought of themselves as "Americans who happened to be Catholic" rather than as "Catholics who happened to be Americans". This confusion about their true fatherland can be our wedge.

Like most Americans, your patient is a sentimentalist. He lives by emotion more than by thought. He's presently feeling like a new bride on her honeymoon with the Enemy. But once the honeymoon is over, the Enemy's policy is almost always to withdraw those special graces He showers on new converts. He wants to toughen them up. That's our opening: Where there are tests, there can be failures, and where a soul has to be toughened up, it can also be softened up.

There's little chance your patient will slide back into conscious unbelief anytime soon. But prospects are very good indeed that you can erode his faith to such an extent that he'll end up even more securely under our influence than a total atheist. How can this can be? Consider the facts:

What happened to him when he believed nothing and knew it? Why, he snapped like a hungry fish right onto the Enemy's hook! Unbelievers who *know* they are unbelievers are in constant danger of questioning their own emptiness and considering the alternative in the clear light of day. But unbelievers who think they believe—these are our securest prey. Right now, No. 66,589/ ADFgm is a believer who knows he's a believer. The goal is to make him an unbeliever who still assumes that he believes.

Therefore, do not attack his faith head-on but rather subvert it, carefully leaving enough residue so that he'll still think of himself as a believer—an "advanced" or "sophisticated" or "nuanced" or "modern" believer, or even a "dissenter". But not an unbeliever. Thus he'll grow increasingly smug, self-satisfied and immune to any more of the Enemy's blandishments.

You see, a little religion often does more good than no religion at all. It's the principle mortals use in treating their diseases. They inject a healthy body with a light dose of the disease germs so that their system builds up a resistance. A little religion is like a mild case of cowpox: It prevents the far deadlier smallpox, the real danger. (Seasoning these creatures with just a touch of faith also brings out some wonderfully interesting flavors once we get them Down Below.)

The Enemy's Son understood the strategy. He told them, "Those who are sick need a doctor, not those who are well. I came to call not the righteous, but sinners, to repentance." Before his conversion, No. 66,589/ADFgm knew he was a sinner. This knowledge put him in jeopardy of seeking out the Doctor for help. Sure enough, he succumbed to that danger, behind Wormhole's back. But if you can convince him even now that "sin" is an outdated concept of premodern psychology, we can recoup all our lost ground, and more.

But how can you keep him from noticing the obvious? Of course he's a sinner. They all are; don't they read the news? Sin is the only dogma of the Enemy's Camp that can be proved just by reading the papers.

Here's where the psychwar mavens in the Public Information Directorate have prepared the way for you. They've insinuated their arguments into the very fiber of the surrounding society and even into his Church. In fact, a surprising number of the creatures' theologians and religious education "experts" believe the only "sin" is to believe in sin!

That's the lynchpin. Knock out sin and the Enemy's whole structure caves in. If there's no sin, there's no need for salvation, and thus the dogmas of the Incarnation, Atonement, Resurrection, Ascension and Second Coming can safely be filed under "mythology".

Furthermore, if he doesn't believe in sin, he won't believe in us. Even if he does believe in sin, he probably won't believe in us; few of them do these days. And even fewer realize the enormous advantage that gives us.

In the past, our strategy was to get them to think about us too much, so that their fear would be stronger than their faith. We had some spectacular successes here, especially in Spain and Salem, and we certainly dined well from the troughs of passionate hate and fear. Ah, what I would give for just a morsel of another Torquemada!

But times change, and enterprises like ours must adapt or die. We now get them to think about us too little, and preferably not at all. This may seem unsound, because when they thought about us more, they were also more inclined to the grand vices, like cruelty. Unfortunately, they found the grand virtues, like courage, equally appealing because they were hardier souls. Since they knew about us, they understood that they were fighting a great spiritual war.

When mortals know they're at war, a kind of Emergency Consciousness arises in them. This can be turned to our advantage, by creating anxiety, but it's a very unstable compound because it can also foster self-sacrifice for a higher cause. When they know they're at war, they live with passion and alertness. They don't greedily demand comfort. There are no yuppies on a battlefield.

But when they believe they're not at war, they become soft. They demand their "rights". They think of the earth not as their training ground but as their home. They confuse wants with needs.

How did we get this immense strategic advantage? Propaganda, Braintwister — it's our metier. Of course they had no evidence to prove we didn't exist. They just drifted with "the spirit of the times" and "the climate of opinion" out of the medieval fire and into the modern fog.

We didn't achieve this all at once. The campaign developed in two steps. First, we got them to disbelieve only in sin, not in sanctity; only in Hell, not in that Other Place. But without the depth of the valley, there can be no height to the mountain, and they soon found themselves on a flat and featureless plain. That's why their mental pictures of God, eternity, angels and saints are all so insipid today: There's no contrast. In the Middle Ages, those images were vivid and powerful, moving pictures. They no longer move men's minds.

If there's a war, there must be an enemy. Who do they think their enemy is? There are only four possibilities:

1. They often used to believe their enemies were concrete human beings. This lie was extremely useful to us when people were passionate enough to know how to hate and stupid enough to ignore the teaching of that inveterate troublemaker Paul, that "we wrestle not against flesh and blood but against principalities and powers."

2. Second, the enemies could be abstract: vice, ignorance, injustice — that sort of thing. That's safely vague. Only scholars can be passionate about abstractions.

3. The third and true possibility, of course, is that they have real, actual spiritual enemies: us.

4. But if they no longer believe that, nor either of the other

options, then the only possibility left is that there are no enemies, and no war, and thus no passion.

And that's where we have them now. Ninety-nine out of a hundred of them never once in their lives get up from bed in the morning with the thought that the forthcoming day will involve a battle in the greatest war of all, and that their Commander is sending them on a mission only they can accomplish. Instead, they think of their planet not as a battle-field but as a bathtub.

Be sure to keep the water tepid. At the right moment, we pull the plug. What delight to contemplate their surprise and terror as they discover they *can* go down the drain!

Your affectionate uncle,

Snakebite

2

ON THE PRIMACY OF THE MIND

My dear Braintwister:

I note that your patient is young, unattached, restless and above all eager to conform to his (pagan) peer group. This is excellent clay.

True, he has believed enough to be baptized, and that infuriatingly mysterious thing called "grace" still clings like an impenetrable odor to his soul. But his mind—well, that is another matter.

Your first step must be not to attack his will but to weaken his mind. Even though the will is nearer to the center of the soul, and is the thing our Enemy wants to possess most of all, yet it grows out of the mind, as a plant grows out of the ground. If we can poison the soil, we can stunt the plant.

Fortunately, most human creatures today are ignorant of this basic principle, so well known to classical thinkers from Socrates to Aquinas. Americans separate theology from morality, mind from will, so much that we can infiltrate their minds— without their even suspecting our presence—much more successfully than we can commandeer their wills.

You see, they believe the absurd dogma (a dogma of their world, not of their Church) that a man's thoughts are his own sacred property, property that not even the Enemy has rights over. Though they are relativists, they think of "freedom of thought" as an absolute. They are skeptical of dogmas, yet they accept this one dogma without proof or argument. Even when they decide to give their lives to the Enemy, they do not easily give their thoughts to Him. They resist all "thought control", even by the Enemy Himself—even though they've been clearly commanded to "bring every thought into captivity" to the Enemy's Son.

Yet, as their own sages tell them, "All that we are is founded on our thoughts." And, "Sow a thought, reap an act; sow an act, reap a habit; sow a habit, reap a character; sow a character, reap a destiny." We can use this principle just as productively as the Enemy can. And the fact that we're far more aware of it than the humans, gives us an advantage.

Your patient's will is still largely aligned with the Enemy's. He has a real desire to "love" the Enemy and his fellow mortals. Were he to die today, he would probably slip through our grasp.

So we must, of course, work toward altering that fundamental bent of his will if we are to hope for final success. We cannot, however, do this directly, against his will. For even Our Father Below cannot change the rules the Enemy so unfairly set (without consultation) even before the beginning of our great struggle—rules He created in the very making of free wills other than His own. But we can hope to change your patient's will indirectly, through the back door, so to speak: the door of his mind.

Even this door cannot usually be rammed head-on. Frontal assaults on faith—planting conscious, deliberate doubts—seldom work. For genuine doubt forces him to ask the question: What is the truth? Thus the flower of rational doubt grows only in the repellently healthy soil of honesty.

Understand that reason is never on our side in the long run. Our aim is always to obscure and darken. It's a perilous task to use little shards of light, reason and argument, to confuse him. It may work in the short run, but the very fact that the mortal is using and trusting reason has the tendency to develop in him an unpleasant urge toward humility, of bowing down to the truth instead of to his own desires, or peer pressures, or fashion—all three of which we can much more comfortably control.

Since he's a typical American youth, he believes, implicitly, that the aim of life is maximum enjoyment. Even though he's not particularly selfish, and lamentable tendencies toward charity exist in his soul, his kindliness is not much deeper than "sharing and caring". The new charity espoused by the Enemy doesn't seem to him, so far, to contradict the old hedonism he believed in before his conversion. He doesn't yet grasp the hard truth that real charity means sacrifice and death to self. He still assumes it means merely gratifying others as well as himself.

Through our influence in the mass media and our penetration of religious instruction even within certain sectors of his Church, we've been able to block from his mind the most important truth of all, the old truth of this death to self and union with God as the *summum bonum* —the greatest good, the meaning of life—and to put in its place a more "modern", more "mature" "sharing and caring" doctrine straight from "Mister Rogers' Neighborhood".

And once we confuse humans about the end, we can much more easily confuse them about the means. Once the goal is obscured, it's almost too easy to lead them into false ways and "lifestyles". (Incidentally, here's yet another psychwar triumph: the implicit reduction of morality to a variety of optional fashions—and they hardly noticed it!)

Always, your work is under the direction of the First Principle of Darkness: Dim the Lights! *Anything* is preferable to truth and light. The moment his mind strays toward asking whether an idea is *true* or *false,* immediately plant suggestions to accept or reject the idea for any other reason: because it is new, or old, or popular, or unpopular, or challenging, or comforting, or left, or right, or even because it makes him happy. We'll even (briefly) tolerate happiness if it's a substitute for truth, because no such "happiness" can possibly last, if it's not *true* happiness.

You already have one powerful lever in his soul: his fanatical desire to avoid being labeled a fanatic. Those Americans who posture themselves as "free" thinkers are often the most sheepish conformists. They fear rejection by men more than rejection by God.

The battle for your patient's soul will be won with surprisingly light attacks on his will if you first darken his mind. Even the Enemy cannot perform an operation without light. And an operation is precisely what the Enemy must accomplish on his soul to free it from us and fit it for that Other Place. Of course you'll want to tempt the patient to jump about on the operating table against the will of the Surgeon; but it's even more effective to tempt him to think he really needs no operation at all.

I notice that no one has ever shown him, bluntly and convincingly, despite his formal religious instruction, that he's a sinner. The term "original sin" connotes to his mind not much more than some curious medieval superstition. At the same time, he knows this is one of the Catholic dogmas. Thus, he's already, in effect, dissenting his way out the church door. Get him to browse through some of those modern theologians who idealize dissent, so he can be confirmed in the habit by giving it a flattering label.

Dissent from any of the Enemy's dogmas is useful to us. It's the wedge by which we can insert more and more doubts later, just as humans insert more and more stones under a lever to lift a heavy object. One of their first scientists said, "Give me a fulcrum for my lever to rest on, and I can move the world." Your patient's first modest act of dissent is your fulcrum by which you can move his whole soul.

For that first wedge is like the first drink, or drug, or cigarette, or affair: It will not be his last. It's the first exception to the rule that all the Enemy's dogmas are infallible; and wherever humans make an exception to a rule, they make a rule of making exceptions. If he thinks, "I will believe everything the Enemy has revealed *except* that medieval superstition of original sin", he is saying, in effect, "I will believe whatever parts of His teaching agree with my opinions, and whatever parts disagree with it, I won't."

Thus he's really erecting a standard above Him, and judging Him by that standard: his mind over the Enemy's. And what he so naïvely considers "his" opinions are usually the fashionable ideas of his age, of which we are the masters. Thus we get to judge the Enemy rather than vice versa, in the court of his soul.

That's why dissent is so remarkably useful to us—not only because all of the Enemy's revealed dogmas are true and useful to them, like a road map for life, and we savor it when they freely choose to tear big pieces out of their maps; but also because it teaches them the crucial habit of judging the Enemy's mind by their own rather than vice versa, playing God to God. That is precisely the great precedent established by Our Father Below. That habit trains them for the very life of Hell, which is precisely "My will be done", and weans them away from the very life of that Other Place, which is "Thy will be done." Once this habit poisons the soil of their mind, it will inevitably poison the plant of their will that springs from it.

And then they're on their way Here Below, just in time for dinner.

Your affectionate uncle,

Snakebite

3

SEX AND THE MEDIA

My dear Braintwister:

To advise you how best to tempt your patient in matters of sexuality—a vast continent for these disgusting creatures—I need to first give you some background.

Our past success on this front is largely the result of two factors. The two may seem contradictory, yet both work for us. The first is that your patient, like most Americans, is a conformist (though he fancies himself a freethinker). He fears being different, eccentric, or (worst of all) "a fanatic", much more than he fears being wicked. The second factor is that the society to which he aspires to conform is in fact a highly elitist society, dominated by a tiny coterie of opinion molders in the media and educational establishments. This elite is now virtually eating out of our claws. It's generations ahead of the masses in matters of morality and religion.

(We haven't entirely succeeded in dominating their politicians, because Americans elect their representatives—but not their educators or media elite. Yet it's not an insurmountable problem because politicians have far less real power than teachers or magazine writers or moviemakers in current American culture, since they must at least appear to be servants of the people. If they don't reflect popular opinion, they're simply not elected.)

Here are some useful statistics on our media clients. Though nearly half of all Americans attend church at least occasionally, fewer than one in 10 of our elite do. Though 72 percent of

Americans think abortion is somehow bad and should be limited, only 3 percent of our elite do. Though seven out of 10 Americans believe there are moral absolutes, only one in 10 of our elite do. Though eight out of 10 Americans believe in a God they will meet and be judged by after death, only one in 10 in our elite do.

See? We've won the teachers, soon we'll have the students. Once you capture the cause, you soon own the effect. And these teachers aren't limited to the classroom; through TV, movies, magazines and music, we've turned the whole society into a classroom. And the lesson plans are written by us.

We have a right to preen a bit over this success, but we should also be realistic and candid. Not only do we have the usual Enemy counterattacks to fend off, but we're also struggling with a contradiction within our own strategy, and if the humans ever sense it, our plans may be ruined.

Here's the problem. On the one hand, we want the human vermin to be bland, egalitarian conformists. Our strategy has been to produce photocopied souls, and we've labored long and hard (and quite successfully) for more than a century now to rid them of the very concepts of excellence, nobility, superiority, hierarchy and authority. Nearly all of them, when they hear those words, react with a negative knee jerk. Their unconscious creed is: What all cannot attain, no one should.

But on the other hand, the masses remain much more traditional, religious and moral in their beliefs than our elite. (Note the statistics above.) We don't want souls to conform to the real majority just yet—not until the majority is ours. You must therefore keep your patient from noticing the contradiction between his egalitarianism and his elitism.

But here's the good news: You'd be amazed how easy this is. Remember our basic principle of keeping his mind and his morals in separate compartments.

The Enemy wants him to be an elitist about ideas and ideals, and an egalitarian about people; to be suspicious and critical of ideas but open and welcoming to all people. Our strategy is to make him just the opposite: an elitist about people and an egalitarian about ideas. Make him think his teachers and scriptwriters are superior people, but also that one idea isn't really superior to another, that all ideas are equal, that there's no objective truth, no real right and wrong, and thus no one has any right to "impose his own values on others". (You simply will not believe how much mileage we've gotten out of *that* hogwash!)

Once again, keep his mind away from noting the self-contradiction in our propaganda, the value judgment that there are no real value judgments, the dogma against dogma.

How can they not notice such an obvious contradiction? They can, Braintwister, they can—especially the well educated ones. The more educated they are, the less they believe in logic and common sense. It's the farm boys and cleaning women whose minds we've been unable to twist.

Really, did you think the sexual revolution of the 1960s just "happened"? No, it was the flowering of a long, deliberate strategy. The basic principle of our approach is a one-two punch: Hit them where they're soft and weak, and at the same time hit them where they're hard and proud—in other words, between their legs and between their ears.

They've always been soft in the reproductive organs, of course. How typical of the Enemy to invent that obscene joke of a "rational animal", to put an angel-like spirit in an ape-like body! But now we've softened their heads too. They've always had trouble obeying the Enemy's law of chastity; but they've never had such trouble understanding it and believing it until now. It's not new that we've tempted them to live promiscuously, but it's thoroughly novel that we've tempted them to justify it, to glorify it, even to sanctify it.

How did we manage it? We had some success with philosophers, playwrights, artists, novelists and poets over the last century, but our campaign really took off with the advent of movies and TV. The secret is the power of images. The humans can put up defenses against ideas, which have to pass the gate keeper of their mind, Reason; but they're weak as water against images. Images sneak in through their unconscious, which is a helpless child.

If we plant the same kind of image in them over and over again through TV and movies, they'll gradually be desensitized. Sex and violence are our two specialties, of course. Our media elite personnel have relentlessly pressured for more. If the sex and violence curve continues at the current rate, we'll have Hell incarnate in their minds in just two more generations. There's nothing, literally nothing, these creatures won't allow. Already, most things the last generation would have regarded as unthinkable are commonplace on TV.

With the movies, it was a two-step strategy. First, their films showed more explicit sexual promiscuity, but within a moral context—"crime and punishment", so to speak. Movies like *Carnal Knowledge, Alfie* and *Shampoo* typify this stage. Then, once the explicit images became commonplace, the sheep were too passive to protest the removal of the moral frame. Their moralists played right into our strategy; they were so hung up on how much flesh was shown that they forgot the lesson the images taught. They were so shocked at overt eroticism, even in a framework of fidelity, that they hardly noticed the snide little smirks for infidelity.

The upshot is that now, nearly every single movie that's made for young people *must* have a dash of nudity, no matter how gratuitous (and of course never, never between married people). And every time a boy first kisses a girl, the next scene always shows them in bed. What a triumph of image propaganda!

The lesson it bores into them unconsciously, like holes bored in the hull of a ship, is so obvious I'm surprised they don't get bored with it: that the normal, the natural, the inevitable corollary of kissing is copulating.

Notice the power of images, Braintwister. Not even a professor could be fool enough to fall for that as an argument. Put it in words, and it's ridiculous. Put it in images, and it's compelling.

Thus we've persuaded them to rationalize their lust, to believe that feeling, not marriage, justifies sex. Most of them don't yet believe in infidelity, but they do believe in fornication. The only strictures they put on copulating are "emotional maturity" and "commitment", which are vague enough for anyone but an infant to claim.

Oh, we've had a field day with their heads. There have been times and places in the past where we've had as much success with their hormones, but never with their heads. That's because never before has a society been so educated, and never before have we so dominated the education industry, especially the extracurricular one, the media.

We've also succeeded in imposing a total media censorship on the one subject that is the most important thing of all in the lives of the majority of the people in the country, but which is never allowed to enter even the most "realistic" movies or public TV shows. I mean, of course, religious faith. Religion is shown occasionally, but from the outside, and never as *true*. The only characters shown as deeply religious are either bigots or sissies.

Though we've undermined their sexual morality, we haven't yet rotted away the rest of their Christian ethics. We've persuaded only a few to accept cruelty, the last bastion of their moral absolutism; but we've succeeded in glorifying it and desensitizing them to it, for example, just by making "slasher" movies fashionable. Wait till they see the next step!

But we mustn't let our love of violence distract us from our main task. Niceness is as useful as nastiness, stamp collecting is as useful as murder, if only it sucks these vermin from the Enemy's grasp. That's the only thing that matters in the end.

The Enemy has this utterly ridiculous thing about repentance, you know. Sometimes I suspect He deliberately allows us to tempt some of the vermin to great sins just so that they'll see them more clearly and repent more strongly, and thus escape our two most deadly nets, pride and self-satisfaction. That supremely troublesome philosopher Thomas Aquinas let out a secret of the Enemy's strategy when he said that just as a doctor may tolerate a lesser disease to free his patient from a greater one, the Enemy often deliberately withholds that loathesome thing He calls "grace" and allows a soul to succumb to our temptation to some clear, external sin in order to free it from pride and bring it to repentance.

The Enemy really will forgive any sin, you know—that is, any sin He can forgive, i.e., any sin that's repented of. So impenitence is what we must aim at, by dulling their consciences to guilt, making them feel more guilty about guilt than about sin.

Your patient does, unfortunately, have something of a conscience. That's our enemy, Braintwister. Conscience is the Enemy's own mouthpiece in the soul. Shut it down at any cost.

Our end, of course, is not simply to inveigle the brutes into bed with each other, but (1) to win their souls through corrupting their society (after all, a "good" society is simply one where it's easy to be good, as one of their more dangerous but fortunately obscure thinkers, Peter Maurin, has said); (2) to corrupt their society through destroying its fundamental foundation, the family, the one place they naturally learn the

Enemy's philosophy of unselfish love, being loved just for who you are, not for what you do; (3) to destroy the family through destroying marriages; (4) to destroy marriages through destroying fidelity, their anchor and glue; (5) to destroy fidelity through the new philosophy of "sexual liberation" and the "sexual revolution"; and (6) to do that through our domination of the media. It's a simple six-step sexual strategy.

One of the most pernicious ideas that can creep into your patient's head is throwing away his TV set. That would burn the bridge by which we march into his heart. But that's an act so radical that few of them are ever capable of it—no junkie likes going cold turkey.

Your affectionate uncle,

Snakebite

4

HOW TO SHOOT CHASTITY IN THE HEAD

My dear Braintwister:

I explained in my last letter how our colleagues have softened up the sexual morality of your patient's society. The field is well cultivated; now sow your seeds. It should be easy for you to suck that softie into our vortex of obsession and confusion. Here's how.

The first principle is always: Dim the Lights! Keep his mind darkened. Those stupid vermin will dance like fleas around issues of sexual morality, complexifying the simplest questions and rationalizing their answers with incredible dexterity—all because we keep their mind off the first and simplest truth: that the Enemy has written the world's simplest sex manual for them, with only two commands in it. First, "be fruitful and multiply". Sex is His invention. Second, "thou shalt not commit adultery". No sex outside marriage, before or after. In it, the more, the merrier.

Nothing could be simpler, and when his eyes turn toward that simple shaft of light from the Enemy's loathsome sun, all our fogs of confusion instantly dissipate. So you must keep his attention focused on anything and everything else—a pair of buttocks, of course, but even ideals will do if necessary. Don't worry if he thinks about moral "values"; just don't let him think about the moral law. Let him fantasize about "virtue" if you must, but for Satan's sake, don't let him look at the light and ask the simple question of what is the Enemy's will.

There are three channels through which this terrible light comes: conscience, Scripture and Church.

You can't kill his conscience. Only he can do that. Souls can commit suicide, but they can never be murdered. But you can blind his conscience by churning up heavy seas of desire and raising heavy rains of rationalization.

A clear mind and a good will are, unfortunately, quite strong enough to conquer and control even passionate desire; but they don't know that any more. Convince him that he's just not strong enough, even with the Enemy's help. Turn his eyes away from the Enemy and onto himself; that's the skeleton key to all the doors. If you can't make him forget the Enemy's promise of help ("grace") altogether, then try to reduce it to a vague generality, not the alarmingly real, specific and present reality we know it is. And use the appeal to hidden pride in making him think he's being very humble to think he's too weak to obey.

Though you can befog his conscience, you can't, unfortunately, change one word of scripture. There it is, right out in public, in the clear, obscene light of day. That's exactly the Enemy's purpose. But you *can* change your patient's "interpretation" of it.

First, making him think of "infallibility" as a bad old word, like "Inquisition". (Of course that makes no sense, Braintwister, but that's exactly your business: to get them to think nonsense. You'll be amazed how eagerly they swallow it if only they read it somewhere.)

If you can't get him to deny infallibility, get him to muddle its meaning, to "nuance" it. (That word is like silicone spray for us!) This will slide it effectively out of his grasp.

Third, there's the Church. That's even more bothersome for us because even if Scripture is obscure, the living, teaching Church is there to clarify it. The same techniques, however, can disarm the Church: thinking of infallibility as a superstition, a myth, or an exaggeration; and "nuancing" or watering down what it clearly says. Always muddy the waters.

You won't be able to tempt him not to think about the Enemy and His law unless you at the same time tempt him to think of something else instead. The obvious candidate is a woman's or a man's body, preferably in fantasy rather than in reality. (Those magazines are so useful there, and not only the pornographic ones but even the fashion magazines; for hardly any real man or woman ever looks that perfect, so that the fantasizer is always disappointed with reality.) But his own desires are as effective a substitute for the Enemy as is another person's body.

When he thinks about his own desires, due to the work of our agents, he, like most Americans, confuses his "needs" with his "wants" and thus is convinced that his great sexual wants equal great sexual needs. Of course this is nonsense; he has water needs, but not sex needs. He'd die without water, but not without sex. But he doesn't want to notice that fact.

But be careful. It can be dangerous to tempt him to ingrown eyeballs and self-scrutiny *at the wrong time.* Our strategy must always be to get them to think of themselves when they're in truth, or in joy, or in true love, or in holiness. Thus we spoil their certainty about truth by turning them to the question: How do I know? We spoil their joy by psychologizing about it. We spoil their love of others by love of self, or love of love. And we spoil their holiness by the awareness of it, which leads to pride.

But when they're sinning, or planning to sin, or being tempted to sin, our strategy must be to tempt them to look at the idol we're putting between their eyes and the Enemy, and not at themselves; at the beauty of the forbidden creature rather than at the ugliness of the state of their own soul that's being addicted and enslaved to it.

It's also useful to plant the suggestion in his mind that sex is really a simple little thing, that the Church has vastly exaggerated the importance of sexual morality. The more obsessed *he* is with sex, the more he'll want to think it's the Church that's obsessed with sex (mortals call that "projection").

It's easy for them to belittle the importance of sexual morality because few of them even understand the meaning of "sacred", and those that do seldom apply it to sex, except in some swoony, ethereal, otherworldly way.

Their "sex education" is purely materialistic and biological. Once sex is thought of as merely a natural, biological act, the Enemy's law about it appears as an alien intrusion rather than as the inner law of its own nature, and the Enemy seems to be making much ado about nothing.

It's amazingly easy to get him to think two contradictory things at once: first, that sex is only biological and the Church idealizes and spiritualizes it, and second, that sex is much more "spiritual" than the Church realizes, since she teaches that the only purpose of intercourse is reproduction. This is a simple lie, of course, but we've arranged for media lies to creep into every home, via TV and newspapers, while the official Church teachings rarely reach further than the Church bureaucracies. Why, even the Pope can't tell them things without the media, and we control most of that.

If he's somewhat sympathetic to "feminists", he may fall for the line that traditional Church teaching about sex is invalid because it came from men, not women (of course, that argument would also invalidate Euclidean geometry!), and because most of that teaching comes from celibates, to boot—as if celibates had no hormones, or as if those who know desire by giving in to it know it better than those who know it by controlling it. That's like saying that only alcoholics really know alcohol. What fun to sneer at their stupidity!

Another technique is to alternate between temptations to pride and despair: unrealistic overestimation and unrealistic underestimation of his power to obey the Enemy. You can do both by getting him to gulp down great globs of guilt, which produces the Freudian reaction against guilt. First, get him to think that sexual sins are the only really serious ones, then, in reaction to that, that they're not sins at all. Never let him see both these two truths at once: that sex is specially sacred, since it is the way the Enemy makes new immortal souls; and that moral responsibility is diminished by strong passion, so that cold, calculating, dispassionate sins are worse than sins of weakness.

Both overdone guilt ("What a great sinner I am!") and underdone guilt ("How innocent I am!") are forms of pride. Never let him see himself as he is: an ordinary, grubby little child.

Peer pressure is incredibly effective on these gregarious, conformist Americans. "Everybody's doing it" is now not only an excuse but virtually a call to arms. It's also easy to make him feel superior to parents and moralists, who seem to him not to realize that "everybody's doing it". After all, they've never lived in a coed dorm, have they? Those benighted dinosaurs just don't realize that virgins are as rare as unicorns today, and just as weird.

You can have fun getting him to think contradictories here again: (1) that those traditionalists are hopelessly idealistic, living in a fool's paradise of past proprieties, and (2) that they're hopelessly pessimistic, down on modern youth, convinced the world is going to Hell in a handbasket. (It's not. It's going to Hell in a Honda.)

Peer pressure is especially effective on the young, who are still forming their identities. We can control peer pressure (through the media and the vague cloud of "fashionableness") much better than we can control the free choice of an individual soul. For one thing, we control most media personnel; for another, fog and clouds and vagueness are our element. It's not for nothing that His Imperial Lowness is called "the prince of the power of the air".

Remember my previous advice about spiritual warfare: don't let him suspect he's at war, that his choices are a matter of life or death. Don't let him think of death. *"Memento mori"* lost many a soul. There are few sins they will commit on their deathbeds. So blind him to the fact that he is on his deathbed as soon as he is born.

Keep his eyes off the principle he knows with certainty from his experience as well as from the Enemy: that obedience always brings happiness and disobedience always brings misery. He has had many past experiences of temptations given in to, and they've all given him guilt, misery and regret. He has also had many past experiences of temptations overcome, and that has always give him joy, peace and gratitude. You wonder how you can keep such a clear truth of experience from him? Just turn his eyes from the past to the future, from the actual to the potential. The more he lives in the future, the more he's ours, for we are the masters of the unreal, and the future is unreal, the not-yet. The Enemy is the master of reality, and lives in the present, and wants them to do the same. But through the work of our agents, we can convince them that "living in the present" really means following every desire and whim in hope of attaining promised pleasure, i.e., living in the future!

Learn from your successes, Braintwister. After triumphs in sexual temptations, apply the same technique in other areas, especially greed for money. The Enemy's Son spoke far more about money than sex, yet the mortals hardly ever worry about greed, only theft. Many have more lust for money than for sex.

With success, you will begin to notice a general shiftiness in your patient, a fear, a hiding, a vague dishonesty that covers his whole life, like a cloud. That's the great effect of unrepented sin. You'll also notice an addictiveness creeping into his whole personality, for addiction to anything makes him an addict, a slave. After sexual addiction, try alcohol. Start with candy, end with drugs.

Above all, keep him away from truth, especially simple, concrete truths like the three reasons to say no to fornication:

1. It can kill you. AIDS.
2. It can kill your marriage. Premarital promiscuity doubles the likelihood of postmarital divorce. (We've kept those statistics well hidden.)
3. It can kill your soul, like any sin.

The Enemy has commanded premarital chastity and postmarital fidelity, with no ifs, ands, or buts. Your job is iffing, anding, and butting.

Your affectionate uncle,
Snakebite

5

ON ABORTION

My dear Braintwister:

Admirable! Not only did you arrange for your patient to jump into bed with that miserable female he's dating, but he even got her pregnant! Best of all, you now have them on the brink of an abortion.

If you can nudge them off that cliff, you may chalk up three scores for our side: two souls partially and one body totally destroyed. What a perfect parody of the "Holy Family" *those* three make! Ah, we do well to be proud of our work, Braintwister—you for obeying my sage advice and I for giving it.

The Low Command will coordinate your efforts with those of Soulsqueezer, assigned to the girl, since you can pressure her most effectively through him. Here are some tips.

Get your patient to think he's being "compassionate" when he worries with her about the "unthinkable" consequences of carrying the pregnancy to term, either keeping the baby or giving him up for adoption. Keep their eyes focused on the burdens involved with alternatives to abortion, but never on abortion itself. *That* must always appear as an escape route.

Get him to magnify, first in his own mind and then in hers, the social stigma she fears from an out-of-wedlock pregnancy—as if all her friends were Victorians! And be sure she believes it would be psychologically impossible to give her baby up for adoption—as if her maternal instincts were too strong to let her son live with anyone else, but not too strong to prevent her from murdering him!

Add the very real fears and follies of an unwanted "shotgun marriage". But keep her mind off the consequences of abortion for her as well as for the baby: the guilt and bitterness, the hardness, the loss of innocence, idealism and romance, the obsessive memories that will come on every anniversary of her baby's death.

Of course, never let either of them use such simple and honest language as that. See to it that they find such comfort in calling it a "fetus" and such horror at calling it a baby that realism and honesty are killed in their soul before the baby is killed in her womb.

And don't forget to magnify the medical dangers of pregnancy and minimize those of abortion, especially the frequency of sterility and frigidity. Our agents have kept such facts well hidden, despite books that document them, for we've seen to it that those books are advertised to, and read by, only the already converted.

Get him to take her to one of those "pregnancy counseling centers" that advertise "choice" but are really feeders for our abortion mills. Be sure they don't stumble into one of those abortion-alternative traps like Birthright. They're more dangerous to our cause than all the arguments in the world.

So you must keep the facts hidden. Remember always the first principle, Dim the Lights. Keep their eyes off the simple, honest question of objective truth, the question of just what abortion *is* and what the "thing" that is poisoned, scalded, or cut limb from limb by abortion is. Never let them call it a "baby".

How, you may wonder? Surely they know it is a baby? Yes, but make them think that calling it a baby would settle the issue (as it would) and close off all "escape" paths (abortion) and thus close their minds. You can even contrive to get them to think that letting a baby live is closed-minded, and murdering it is open-minded!

If you can't keep that loathsome word "baby" out of their minds, don't let them think of it as *their* baby, only *hers.* Stir up as much fear and strife between them as you can. That will keep the waters agitated, so that they won't look at the two obvious facts: (1) that it *is* a baby and (2) that it is *their* responsibility, *their* baby. She must see it as *her* "problem" or possession. We'll be sure that soulsqueezer keeps up the clap-trap about her "right to control *her* body and her life".

Now is the time to use those clichés they've always heard about "values" being "personal" (code for relative, arbitrary). You may even get them to think of objective reality itself as subjective, of truth as a creation of the human mind. There are many philosophers and many more sociologists and psychologists who have softened their brains this way already. They may never have heard the names Kant and Comte and Dewey, but their ideas have trickled down into their minds since kindergarten.

Once you can get them to disbelieve in objective truth, anything becomes possible. They don't realize how powerful a lever that is. They think of that question as too abstract and technical to make a difference to their lives. Ha! As if the light in an operating room were too abstract to make a difference to the operation!

Be sure you appeal to "compassion"—but not for the baby, of course. They can't see the baby. You'd be surprised how much that helps. It's hard for them to feel real compassion for someone they can't see, or who looks different from them (like a very young unborn baby). This also conditions them to judge by appearance and unconsciously to look on the severely handicapped as only half human.

But be sure they just love baby seals, whales and snail darters. And let them wallow in orgies of harmless love for people they've never met and cannot help, victims of oppression half the world away. Not only does this give us pleasure, to laugh at their stupidity, but it also satisfies that moral itch the Enemy planted in them. Fantasy is quite harmless to us, even idealistic and moral fantasy. Only hard facts count: character, choice, deed.

Control their pronouns, so that they never call their baby a "he" or a "she" but only an "it". You see, we can manipulate them through words. Their words are *supposed* to mirror their thoughts, and their thoughts are *supposed* to mirror reality, according to the Enemy's intention; but we can get them to twist their thoughts by twisting words, and to twist reality by twisting thought. We work backward.

The reason this works is that they need holding-places in their language for their thoughts, or else those thoughts, without verbal anchors, will just drift away. And if they have no holding-places in their thoughts for certain realities, those realities will no longer be believed in, and reality itself will start to drift away from them. In other words, the very drift that they will experience in Hell can begin on earth through the manipulation of words.

Surely you remember the spectacular success we had in Nazi Germany using this principle. Why, if the Nazis hadn't already coopted the phrase, we would have led them to call *abortion* "the final solution".

Now, to answer your question about that moment of searing pain you had when the two of them were "making their baby". You wonder how a sin could give us pain instead of sheer pleasure. Well, unfortunately, it gives *them* pleasure, and therefore it gives *us* pain. Hell has so far been unable to invent any sin that gives them no pleasure at all (with the possible exception of envy). We have to make do with what we have, and that means using the Enemy's own inventions, though we turn them against Him. Pleasure is His invention, and He glued it to the sex act so tightly that we can break that glue only in extreme cases.

But there are more-than-adequate compensations. Be thankful that the act was preceded by such delicious sins as disobedience, dishonesty, self-will, and refusal even to attempt self-control; and followed by guilt, disappointment and confusion in such great waves that we could surf on them. These two feasts of pleasure for you were surely worth the one moment of pain sandwiched between them, just as that brief ecstasy for them was nothing compared to the great pain and harm to their souls that came before and after.

Just think, Braintwister, what a horrible time tempters have who are assigned to faithful married people who time after time enact their disgusting little animal ecstasies within the secure framework of the Enemy's law, like a great painting surrounded by a great frame. Those poor devils have none of the ghoulish glee you had at the two little animals running from the Enemy in rebellion before, and in shame after, the deed. Those poor devils feel nothing but pain at the animals' unmitigated love, especially if they hold nothing back and do not even contracept. How vulgar and tasteless the Enemy is, to create immortal souls in such a crudely animal way, and amid such pleasure! How we relish it when we can pervert *this* plan of His, which we hate so much. Love—how every form of it sticks in our gullet and chokes us!

You did well not to rest on your laurels once you had gotten them to fornicate, but immediately pressed your advantage by tempting them to abort. See to it that they put the two deeds in the same category and do not acknowledge that the second destroys life while the first produces it. "If we did the first, we can do the second", must be their train of thought.

Just as one lie leads to another, to cover it up, so any one sin leads to another. You have them on the slippery slope now. Redouble your efforts. Never relax! Hell has no vacations and tolerates no failures. If you can foresee and forestall all repentance which would undo the Gordian knot you are tying, you will be able to twist your tendrils round and round their souls endlessly.

Hell has caught many a soul through the slippery slope. One drink leads to more, to a habit, to an addiction, to a ruined life, to despair and to us. Trying pot leads to trying stronger stuff, and to crime or suicide or an overdose, and they get off the slide into a pool of fire. Lust leads to fornication, fornication leads to abortion, a killed baby leads to a killed conscience and to bitterness or despair.

Unfortunately, the Enemy provides many exits from our slide, many opportunities to repent. We can't close those exits. We can't expect to catch all sliders. But we *can* expect to catch some. Not all who start with small sins end in Hell, but all who end in Hell start with small sins.

We've succeeded in social temptation as well as individual temptation by the slippery slope principle. A society that practices and justifies abortion is already well advanced down the slope. The next step is euthanasia and infanticide, of course. Soon—far sooner than they think—"Brave New World". Already they have test-tube babies and surrogate mothers, all in the name of "compassion".

How wonderful to hear them justify abortion in the name of "compassion". They'll find out how much compassion the god of abortion has when Moloch comes again! How we howled with delight when Carthage invited him to dine on soft baby flesh and warm baby hearts! We even got many of the Enemy's Chosen People to worship Moloch, in an orgy of ecumenism. Many of Israel's successors, in the Enemy's Church, are following the same path. Fortunately for us, "those who do not learn from the past are condemned to repeat it".

Once Moloch is unleashed, their society is doomed. For abortion, which is his worship, is not just one isolated sin, but an attack on life itself. Our death-road into this society is already a superhighway. We have made the safest place in the world, a mother's womb, the most dangerous. We have turned this natural place for love, acceptance and nurturing into a place for resentment, violence and a war on children.

The heart of Moloch's triumph is this: Those who abort almost inevitably believe one of two premises, either of which, if consistently applied, is a straight road to Hell: (1) that objective truth does not matter (for the objective truth is, of course, that abortion is a mother's murder of her baby) or (2) that I am my own and others' master, that if I will to kill, I will kill. "*My* will be done" and "Better to reign in Hell than serve in Heaven" — the most two profound sayings ever invented, by You Know Who!

Your affectionate uncle,

Snakebite

6

IS GOING TO CHURCH REALLY IMPORTANT?

My dear Braintwister,

What a wonderful triumph. You've managed to persuade your patient and his "sex partner" to abort the product of their "love". How delicious to contemplate the paradox of "love" resulting in death rather than life!

Better yet, you didn't rest on your laurels but went right to work to follow up your advantage with some preventative maintenance against repentance by strongly stirring the tides of his soul in the direction of drifting away from church attendance. Another delicious paradox: We can use their very spiritual diseases to drift them away from the only Doctor who can cure them! I'm happy to see that you clearly realize the close connection there can be between a moral crisis and church attendance, and also that you see the need to keep him from seeing that connection.

One of the Enemy's simplest and smartest sons, G. K. Chesterton, saw the connection clearly. When asked why he joined the Church, he replied, "To get my sins forgiven". If your patient ever plainly faces the question: "Why am I no longer going to church?", his reason may wake up and convince him he's been a fool, and is on the road to being a damned fool—a fool to flee the very thing he needs all the more now.

The Enemy is indeed, as His Book says, "a consuming fire". Keep your patient at the outer edges of that fire, where it burns. If he turns (repents) and plunges into the heart of that fire, he'll find that it's just the oppose of earthly fire: The closer he gets to its center and source, the less it burns and the more it heals.

I assume you know strategic principle No. 77: *Before* they sin, make them think only of the Enemy's mercy, not His justice; *after* they sin, make them think only of His justice, not His mercy. The Enemy wants exactly the opposite. If we can get them to think only of justice after they've sinned, they'll think of punishment, thus of fear, thus of avoiding fear, thus of turning away from the Doctor. Justice is His diagnosis, mercy is His cure. Keep them from the cure by never letting them connect the diagnosis with the cure.

One reason we have a lot to fear from the simple fact of regular church attendance is that this is virtually the only public testimony to their faith that any of them are ever required to give today. It is a litmus test, a loyalty test. That's why it was so important for our agents to infiltrate the religious education programs, to persuade them to teach only this one thing about the Church: that "the Church is people"; that you don't "go to church", you "are church". We've made them see these two ideas as mutually exclusive rather than inclusive, and we've discredited the simple "old faithful" idea of "going to church" as some old hangup, guilt trip or superstition.

We've been helped here enormously by the media's perversion of Vatican II's "new" definition of the Church as "the people of God". (Of course it isn't really new.) We've gotten them to think of the Church clean contrary to the actual teachings of Vatican II (but who reads those?), as a kind of religious social club, a merely horizontal, human thing. We've reduced the vertical, supernatural dimension to something subjective, and reduced faith to something about feelings rather than about facts. Instead of the hard, objective idea of Church, we've substituted a soft, subjective, squooshy one. The Church Militant has become the Church Mumbling; the Church Invincible has become the Church Insipid.

You can appeal to his chronological snobbery and his disdain of the simple truisms everyone knows about the Church. For instance:

Make him scorn the simple idea that the Church is a building. Of course it's more than that, but it's that too, and we want him to forget that, because that building is as threatening to us as an abortion clinic is to an unborn baby. Why, the things that go on in that building! It makes me wrench with pain and retch with disgust whenever I think what happens in that confessional and on that altar!

The sense of the sacred, and of a sacred place and time—a sense that is nourished by that building and by his ritual attendance in it—must be eradicated from his consciousness. We are now in the final stages of our modern campaign to eradicate first each sacred thing and then the sense of the sacred itself. Life, death, sex, the body, a woman's womb—few of them have the slightest inkling of what it means to call these things "sacred" now. If we can desacralize even the Church, the only remaining step will be to desacralize their very idea of the Enemy Himself. Then we will have screwed down the manhole covers on them and squashed them into a flat, gray, egalitarian world that is almost as boring as Hell itself.

(You will, of course, burn this letter as soon as you read it.)

The public testimony inherent in going to church every Sunday—the thing every child knows is important—we must make him ignore. The idea that going to church is a kind of Rubicon must be dismissed as silly. Soon there will be no Rubicons left, no clear, specific acts to differentiate the children of the Enemy from the children of Our Father Below. We've gotten their whole society madly rushing into an orgy of egalitarianism, running from the odium of distinctiveness as from the smell of a skunk.

They used to take pride in their distinctiveness. Now they're embarrassed at it. So it's pitifully easy for us to tempt them to ignore or scorn anything distinctively Catholic. Let them first be Protestantized (within the Catholic Church), then dechristianized into a vague theism, then humanized into a smart secularism with a fashionable veneer of vague religiosity. Be sure you keep that veneer: It's our best inoculation against the real thing. Never let him realize he's drifted away from the Enemy Himself, or he may wake up in a sudden fit of reason and repentance.

The sacrifice of time it takes to go to church is a deliberate act of choice to give something precious (a little of one's lifetime) to the Enemy for no earthly, practical reason. That is extremely dangerous to us. We must blur the distinction between sacred time and secular time, between "their" time and the Enemy's time. Persuade your patient that by not giving one hour a week to the Enemy by church attendance, he's really giving all his time to the Enemy. (The same holds true of money.) This will salve his conscience and at the same time it really means that he will sacrifice no time (or money) to the Enemy. You know, "pray, pay and obey" was really a pretty powerful program for the Enemy, when you come to think of it. But we've gotten it universally laughed at because we've stopped them from thinking about it. The Dim the Lights Principle again.

If you can't keep his body from going to church, at least stop his soul: pervert his motives. Get him to go for any other reason than an act of obedience and worship to the Enemy. Let him go not to give but to get something: comfort, or good feelings, or fellowship. He'll soon stop going, for he can find those things more easily in a bar. If he must go to give and not to get, make him go to give to other people, not to the Enemy. Let him go to church to please his family. We can even use dangerously virtuous motives like that one to prevent greater dangers, just as the Enemy often tolerates lesser vices to prevent greater ones like pride.

If he does go to church, don't let him focus on the Enemy's Son or His Real Presence in the Eucharist. Arrange for the tabernacle to be moved to one side of the building, and its Inhabitant will soon follow to one side of his consciousness.

Terrible, terrible things go on in that tabernacle and on that altar and in that confessional. Oh, the pain, the fear, the powerlessness we feel there! Keep them away from that dreaded building at any cost, foul or even fair.

Here are two equally effective traps to keep them from both Confession and Communion. They are the same two traps that will eventually keep them out of Heaven: pride and despair. They are opposites, but it does not matter which one we use: The only thing that matters is whether a thing leads to the Enemy or to Our Father Below. All else is relative, a mere means to that final end.

You can induce despair by getting him to see the Church as a museum for saints rather than as a hospital for sinners, and making him think he's not good enough for such holy society. In fact, of course, the only qualification for joining the Church is to be *bad* enough, just as the only qualification for entering a hospital is to be sick enough.

You can induce pride by the very same vision of the Church but the opposite vision of himself, as worthy rather than unworthy of this "saint society". You see, once you get him to see the Church as the "saint museum" you've got him; once you've captured his thoughts, you've captured his soul. For either he will see himself as unworthy of the saint-museum—and then despair keeps him out—or as worthy of it, and then pride keeps him out. Pride apparently lets him in, but it really keeps him out just as effectively as despair does. For even though he enters the door, he really isn't in, because the only door through which anyone's soul can enter the Church is the little low door of humility and repentance, the door only the child can enter, as the Enemy's Son so disgustingly said.

Twist his brains, squash his vision, dim the lights! Don't let him see the Church as the awfully big thing it is, spread out in history, rich with saints and sages and martyrs. The little church in his neighborhood must never be seen as the same Church as *that* Church, or the same Church as the Church in Heaven, full of "witnesses" who are watching his earthly struggles right now through heavenly windows. (Don't let him read Hebrews 11 and 12:1.) Don't let him connect the Church of history, the Church of Heaven, and the Church in Purgatory with the dumpy little church on his corner and those dumpy little people crawling in and out like ants. Don't let his eyes be opened like the eyes of Elisha's servant, when he suddenly saw, surrounding the army of Israel's enemies, the army of the Enemy's angels, with horses and chariots of fire (2 Kings 6:15–17). That vision is almost as deadly to us as the vision of the Enemy's face itself.

Other popular perversions of the idea of the Church are the twin errors of Individualism and Collectivism. We've gotten many Protestants suckered into Individualism, and many Catholics suckered into Collectivism with that wonderful magic word "community". When that verbal button is pushed, a knee-jerk reaction goes off in their feelings, a kind of hazy, honeyed happiness, a "warm puppy" feeling in place of the terrible truth of what the Church is: the Enemy's Son's own Body.

Don't let him read Paul, or even C. S. Lewis, or he may discover that the Church, like an organism, is one precisely because its organs are many and different and working for the same end, and is many precisely because it is one in its source of life and in its ultimate goal, just like a body whose blood and energy both unify and at the same time differentiate all its organs. What a horribly obscene invention of the Enemy— the organism. But thanks to our agents, such organic ideas are now labeled "reactionary" or "mystical" and have been replaced by wishy-washy wobblings about "compassion" and "caring" and "community" and "concern" and "consensus". Let those little foxes of innocuous and vacuous c-words run through the Enemy's vineyard, the Big C (Church), and eat all the grapes that could be made into the dangerously intoxicating wine of the old vision that saints lived for and martyrs died for with joy and love and passion and fire in their eyes.

Get him to think of the Church's saints as fanatics, and to despise fanaticism above all else. Thus you will get him to despise lovers without realizing it, for lovers are fanatics (both the earthly and heavenly kinds of lovers).

I know it is painful for us to admit and face those terrible truths, but we must be realistic if we are to win souls for Our Father Below. I hope you can steel yourself to endure the pain of seeing the truths you keep your patient from seeing. If so, you will be rewarded by a feast of "soul food" forever.

Your affectionate uncle,

Snakebite

7

WHAT HAS THE LOWERARCHY
DONE TO THE LITURGY?

My dear Braintwister,

I see you couldn't keep your patient from attending church altogether, despite the excellent advice in my letter. In that case, you'll need some briefing on how we've managed to defuse what goes on in that awful place and how you can go with our flow when he's there. Lucky for you, we've been remarkably successful at smoothing your way, infiltrating the very liturgical heartland of the Enemy.

In my last letter I explained the connection between sexual temptations (in which you have had such great success) and liturgical temptations. I showed you how you could use either guilt or shamelessness, despair or pride to keep him insulated from Confession and Communion. Here's a second connection between bad sex and bad liturgy which none of them know about except the insiders, and they're all afraid to say it. Here's one of the Church's dirty little secrets that explains how we've been able to get inside the liturgy.

Why do you suppose we've succeeded so totally in turning all the humanly invented words and music that surround the Enemy-invented fact called the Mass into such a feeble, flaccid thing? It's simple: The limp-wristed liturgies were designed by limp-wristed liturgists.

No one wants to admit it, but all the clergy know it. The laity would be amazed and scandalized if they knew how many of them were gay, at least in orientation. And the establishments, the administrations, the organizations, the middle management powers that be—why do you think they're so desperately afraid of "confrontation", so obsessed with being nice and well-liked, so confined to "compassion"? Why do you suppose so few of them dare to act like men? Because so few of them are.

The proportion of gays, active or dormant, is even larger, much larger, among liturgists than among the clergy as a whole. That's why the new liturgy is so tepid and timid and tedious. Have you ever heard a single congregation anywhere in the world at any time in the last 25 years ever sing any one of those flat, unmusical "responsorial psalms" with any passion at all? And yet they keep feeding them this tepid, Laodicean pap, neither hot nor cold.

They've gotten the most powerful and dramatic thing in the world—the ritual murder of the Son of God to save souls from Hell—to sound like a Barry Manilow song or a Rod McKuen poem. "There's Power in the Blood" has become "Listen to the Warm"! And they haven't the foggiest idea that most of it comes from messed up sexuality.

Some time I'll brief you more fully on how even theological "dissent" comes largely from that source—and not just in moral theology but in dogmatic theology as well, since the two are very closely connected. Those who are obsessed with their unrepented sexual misbehavior certainly don't want a literally divine, literally resurrected Christ around, or an authoritative Church, or even objective truth, and certainly not a real Hell. But the Enemy's Son clearly believed and taught all these things. So His authority has to be undermined, by undermining the historical accuracy of the Gospels. So even the popularity of Lower Criticism (which they call Higher Criticism, just as they call the saddest among them "gay") is largely due to the need to rationalize their sexual sins. But none of them dare to say that, or they'd be pilloried as Puritans and witch hunters and homophobes by the media, which are securely ours.

The effects on the liturgy have been incredible. Why, many bishops would sooner give permission for a million murders than for one Latin Mass. I mean this literally: Some fudge on abortion but hate and fear the Latin Mass more than they fear us! But this is not as all-important as the Traditionalists think. They could be bored at the old Mass too.

From our point of view, the dangers of drama and the uses of dullness are immense. The Enemy's Son knew this. He was never dull. Everyone who met him was "amazed", whether friends or enemies or undecided. But no one is amazed at the Mass any more. How did we accomplish this?

By remembering that images educate. Dull music, dull translations, dull sermons, and above all a dull priestly tone of voice, all speak a message louder and clearer than any explicit words, argument, or propaganda could ever speak: that this thing, this Mass, this salvation, this Savior, is *dull!* That flinging open Heaven's gates by martyring the Creator is no big deal! Nothing could make them *think* that; they're not that stupid. But a limp liturgy makes them feel it.

They need not just happiness but joy. The Enemy made them that way. If they don't find it in Church, they'll seek it elsewhere (probably in sex), and learn to think in these categories, our categories: Spirit (joyless) vs. Flesh (joy); Church (dull) vs. World (interesting); Religion (boring) vs. Sex (fascinating); Piety (sissified) vs. Sin (strong).

Second, we've performed a sacradectomy, an operation on their soul to remove a whole organ, the sense of the sacred. That's what the liturgists are ultimately up to with their new liturgy: assisting at that operation—(though they usually sincerely think just the opposite, because they've already lost the sense themselves). The awe, the wonder, the worship, the astonished silence before the Mystery, the Fear of God—they've killed all those horrible beasts themselves, Braintwister! What work they've saved us!

The whole human race used to have this sense of the sacred, of course. As intuitively as they knew they were mortal, they knew that birth and death and sex and family and worship and the sky and music and language were sacred. But their society has desanctified all these things by now, even death. Yes, even death, Braintwister! I know it's hard to believe how gullible and stupid they can be. That's why Our Father Below is so much more realistic than the Enemy, who still loves the silly vermin.

Our agents have succeeded in getting those who bemoan the loss of the sacred and seek to restore it labeled as "conservatives". In politics, where that word belongs, it is not necessarily the kiss of death; but in the Church, where it doesn't belong, that "c-word" is worse than cancer. Our propagandists have even succeeded in popularizing the picture of "conservatives" as gray and gloomy when of course the truth is the exact opposite: they want to restore the old Glory, while the "bright, new" liturgy (like the new theology) is really insufferably dull and old before its time, like the liberals themselves.

Third, we've destroyed their sense of ceremony. This is not as strong or directly dangerous as the sense of the sacred, but close. They now think of ceremony as something silly, superficial and fussy. But they didn't think that when they were children. A child naturally invents a funeral ceremony when he buries a dead pet. He instinctively realizes that ceremony smooths over life's rough spots by specifying what to say and do; that ceremony makes you bigger, connects you with the past and even with something cosmic, and teaches you to subordinate yourself and your personality to something greater. (Don't ever let them read Von Hildebrand's *Liturgy and Personality* on this.) But when they get older, they listen not to their deep heart but to their shallow society, and *we* control *that*.

There's very little left in their society to feed their innate sense of ceremony, so it just withers and dies. In some of them, it's so dead that if they ever did happen on a great liturgy, they'd hate it. In others, the sense is dormant, so we have to be sure it's never fed. That's why so much effort has gone into fostering fear of the Latin Mass, Gregorian chant, Palestrina, and the old hymns, and why we didn't rest till we got the Anglicans to revise their Book of Common Prayer. (Be sure to do all you can to discourage any connection or reunion there: We certainly don't want millions of Catholics using that old masterpiece!)

We've made religious ceremony seem embarrassing to them by making their liturgy sound "churchy" without sounding sacred. The old liturgy sounded sacred without sounding churchy; naturally sacred and not embarrassingly churchy; not sissified but strong and proud and high and holy. Now, it sounds weak and embarrassed and flat and secular.

Fourth, we've gotten them to forget or fudge the very center of the liturgy: the Enemy's Son has been moved to the periphery, both physically (when the tabernacle is moved to the side) and spiritually (when humanistic liturgies focus on some abstract idea of "community" instead of the alarmingly present Enemy).

Here are two reasons why the Eucharist is such a danger to us, in addition to the obvious ones. First, it teaches them to walk by faith, not by sight. They can't see the Enemy's Son there, so they have to believe it on the authority of the Church—another idea too deadly for us to endure. There are awful things around them all the time: the Enemy, and His Son, and

His Spirit, and the saints and the angels. We must persuade them to reduce Reality to Appearance. Once they begin to do that with the Eucharist, the door is open to doing the same with those other awful things.

Second, we've been making subjectivists out of them for centuries now, but the Eucharist stands in our way, for it teaches them to worship the real, objective Presence. It turns them outward. We need to turn them inward, give them ingrown eyeballs, confuse faith with feeling, objective fact with subjective interpretation. We've popularized slyly subjective slogan words like "nuancing" and "contextualizing" and "contemporary hermeneutics" because they'll fall for almost any four-syllable fudge-words if only they come from theologians.

Paradoxically, the old liturgy, so impersonal and objective, fostered great personal passion and devotion. The new liturgy tries to exalt people, feeling, subjectivity and community, but it forgets that every one of those things flourishes only when it's forgotten or given away. But we don't let them be taught that old truth any more.

Finally, the new liturgy is a triumph of elitism masquerading as populism. In the name of populism, our liturgical elite have taken over. Our "liturgical experts" have invented a liturgy that only a professional liturgist could ever love, and forced it on the people in the name of populism! One wag said that the Enemy saw that the American Church lacked persecutors so He gave her liturgists.

The real test of a liturgy, of course, is ordinary people. Can a liturgy move a miner, a grandmother, a child, a peasant? The old did; the new doesn't. The secret is that these liturgical "populists" really despise the opinions of ordinary people, just like their liberal counterparts in politics, just as Marx despised the masses. The "experts" are simply snobs, but they've succeeded in pinning the label of snob on their opponents, the simple folk who loved the old liturgy and howled when it was stolen from them. What a wonderful job of reversing the roles of victim and victimizer! (We do the same with rapists and their victims in court time after time.)

The great practical danger to watch out for now is that your patient will overcome the obstacles we invented and worship the Enemy by a sheer act of will, unaided by the sense. This has often happened. We go to all the trouble of de-Catholicizing the liturgy, so they worship like good Protestants! A second danger is that the dullness drives him away so clearly that he knows he's "out" and may deliberately decide to come "in" at some future date. Drifters inside are more safely in our hands than drifters outside, because the "insiders" don't know they're drifting, while the outsiders do. I cannot overemphasize the importance of the First Principle: Whatever you do, Dim the Lights!

Your affectionate uncle,

Snakebite

8

ON LITURGICAL MUSIC

My dear Braintwister,

If you're wondering why your Great Uncle Snakebite would devote an entire letter to talking about liturgical music, then you haven't read the old books. The ancients knew that music is one of the most powerful forces in human life, even though they had only a little bit of music, and quite primitive. The moderns have forgotten the power of music, though their lives are cram-full of it. Well, what they don't know can indeed hurt them. This letter is to make sure you know the hidden powers of music so that you can tailor your strategy with your particular patient to our general work in their society.

How well did the ancients know the hidden power of music? Plato based his whole "ideal" society, in *The Republic,* on its educational system, and he based the whole educational system on music as its first step. He also said that if his ideal society ever came into existence, it would eventually erode first through a decay in music.

The ancient Chinese emperors used to walk through each of the cities in their realm listening to the music the citizens sang and played. If it was bad music, the emperor took the trouble to send his officials to check on the people's social, economic, sexual, religious and moral affairs; but if it was good music, they were left alone to govern themselves. The emperor knew that music was the antenna of the soul.

One twentieth-century writer proved that every social revolution in modern times was preceded by a musical revolution. Music is a prophet. But humans don't listen to their prophets. Being a prophet is a thoroughly non-profit business among them.

The reason music moves them so powerfully and hiddenly is that it bypasses their reason. It sneaks directly into their souls through underground passageways, like water through soil. We have to expend such tremendous effort and invent such devious strategies to put conscious ideas into their minds because ideas have to pass those two unbearably troublesome censors, reason and will, the gatekeepers at the front door of their souls. But music sneaks in the back door. It's not censored by reason. They don't think about it; they just feel it. Not one of their philosophers has ever explained it or fit it into a system.

Even more, some music touches not only the feelings but even the deep center of the soul, the root from which grow both the branches of feeling and reason. That's why Plato wanted musical teaching first: to prepare the soul by nonrational harmony and beauty for the later, rational harmonies of reason and virtue, like soil being fertilized for a crop. If we can corrupt the fertilizer, we corrupt the soil and thus corrupt its crop.

For another thing, music has a cosmic connection. Few moderns and fewer Westerners understand this, but some ancients did and many Orientals do. Confucianism and Hinduism, in different ways, both see the linkage of musical harmony with social harmony and cosmic harmony. But we've taught the modern West to treat that idea like corn flakes.

We've also made them forget the old story that music was the language the Enemy used to create the world, was the language of Eden, and will be the language of Heaven, the universal language. We've also gotten them to forget the mystics' favorite book, the Song of Songs, and even if they pay attention to it, they forget the title. There's hardly a sane, feet-on-the-ground thinker in their world who understands that the world was made in music, not music in the world. We've let secrets like that out only to the pseudo-mystics, neo-pagans, romanticists, New Agers and little foxes in their world, to discredit the idea through guilt-by-association.

Hell has been very practical about music. All we Hellions of course pride ourselves on our practicality. But to be practical we need to know theory first. That's why I've told you all these principles. Plato's principle, especially, is useful: If we corrupt their music, we corrupt their lives, and by such hidden paths that they never suspect the causes and never attack them.

One not-at-all unworthy path, of course, is Satanic rock music. We've let the Satanists blow their own cover because we then get a nice side effect: another guilt-by-association. Because of a few Satan-pushers, a few more drug-pushers, and a lot more sex-pushers among rock groups, millions of the Enemy's most serious followers fear or sneer at the whole genre of rock music. In itself this is not important, except that it deprives them of much natural fun and outlets for adolescent nervous energy, which goes underground, where we can twist it. But more directly, it often makes the critics be or seem like uptight snobs, repressed wimps, self-conscious sissies, or finger-wagging doomsters.

Music is the Enemy's field, of course; He invented it. That's why it hurts us so. But one of our most successful forays into this painful field has been—believe it or not—liturgical music. We've had more success, in some ways, there than with rock music, for Satanic rock is passionate and evil, while their modern liturgical music is insipid and "good"; thus they learn, unconsciously but effectively, to associate passion and energy with evil, and goodness with dullness. This is an invaluable association, for they can't keep at anything for long if it's dull and passionless. The Enemy made their psychic engines to run on the fuel of joy and passion, and if they don't find any of that in the Enemy's stuff, they will inevitably turn to ours. (Music is like sex that way.)

We've hoodwinked the new liturgists and musicologists to hate and fear and call "elitist" that powerful old Church treasure of hymns, and they believe they're being popular and populist when they push on the people their own unmusical music that no one ever sings, or ever will, with any passion — except in charismatic communities, of course; those people will sing anything with gusto, even a laundry list.

We've succeeded in arranging this braintwisting "reverse populism" through ideologizing their music. Ideology is a field we control, for we invented it; music is the Enemy's field and invention. So when we get them to ideologize music, we win.

The process was simple, a matter of two words: the all-purpose sell-word, "new", and the all-purpose sneer-word "old". You won't believe how eager these animals are to let catchwords substitute for thinking! Of course, some of the old music was ugly too, but nearly all of the new stuff is. And if it's not ugly, it's at least limp and harmless. It makes some of them feel "nice" (the new "Battle Hymn of the Republic" is "Have a Nice Day") but it will never make them feel awed, or even odd.

There's danger in the old hymns. I once lost — I mean, I know a demon who lost — a soul through the prayers of his mother, who had developed the dangerous habit of continual prayer only because she kept a hymn tune in her head all day. And a tune brings the words as a whistle brings a dog. Keeping a tune in their heads is much easier for those animals than keeping an idea there. Sometimes they can't keep a tune *out* of their heads all day, especially singing commercials (which, of course, are one of Deep Hell's proudest inventions).

We've lost souls who walked into cathedrals and heard Palestrina. You won't believe how many ex-atheists say Bach alone convinced them there is a G . . . well, you get the picture. Don't let them hear the old stuff. We've got to make them knee-jerk out the word "repressive" whenever they hear the word "tradition". You'll be amazed how easy this is. They hate to think and love to free-associate instead.

We also must not let them be really ecumenical and discover some of those powerful old Protestant hymns. Keep their theology Protestant and their music Catholic, not vice versa. In Hell, Protestants dance and Catholics sing. In Heaven, Protestants teach Catholics to sing, and Catholics teach Protestants to dance.

Why, most Protestant denominations would have lost half their members in two generations if they'd had only the music Catholics have today. Calvin won cold souls (like his own) through his theology, but Luther won hot souls (like his own) through his hymns.

Of course we must foster the generation gap, and rivalry between the old sentimentalists and the new secularists, between "Mother Dear, O Pray for Me" and "Let Us Build the City of God". The wonderful irony of this is that neither side realizes that what Mother Dear is praying for is precisely to build the City of God! But all the sentimentalists want from her is a cure for their arthritis, and all the secularists want is to elect progressive politicians.

What's dangerous to us, especially in liturgy, and more especially in music, is for gaps like that to be bridged—e.g., by music that combines the high and holy with the meek and lowly, the simple and popular with the great and glorious.

Many of the old hymns did just that, and they cut us like knives. The new ones are flat as noodles.

Like all powerful things, music is tricky: hard to get right and easy to get wrong, in opposite ways. Sometimes the musical technique is so bad, so ignored, that it loses all its power and produces only embarrassment. Other times, so much attention is devoted to technique that liturgy turns into performance. That's why we just love a succession of new songs, as we have now in most Catholic churches—"the liturgical fidget", as C. S. Lewis called it.

Of course, the only songs that can ever solve the above dilemma are the old songs, for it takes time to master a song to the point where attention need no longer be focused on technique. Music is like planting: It takes time to grow. So we keep them at the self-conscious liturgical fidget forever, endlessly pulling up the old plants and planting new ones, and nothing ever takes root. They feel like trained animals with new hoops to jump through every week.

You may wonder why their new liturgical music, like their new translations of the Bible, sound so much like committee reports and so little like poetry, and how we could have put that trick across. Well, their real religion is Americanism, i.e., equality: a bland, blind, gray goo. What delicious irony if we can get them to think Heaven is like that—all mixed up together. They're close to that now: they identify distinctions with discrimination, and hierarchy with snobbery! They blend the secular and the sacred, the earthly and the Heavenly, the low and the high; and this means, of course, not that the low is exalted but that the high is diminished. That's why their music sounds like conversation. In Ireland, even their conversation sounds like music. (How I hate that place!)

If we can bring them one more step, to hate not only hierarchical order but all order, structure, reason, *logos* — then we've made them hate the pre-incarnate Son of the Enemy Himself, because that's just what He is from the beginning: the *logos*. We can't hurt Him directly, but we can harm His traces, and we can begin in music, if we use Plato's principle.

The mortals who have had near-death-experiences often hear Heavenly music. *They* know music is not merely earthly, like money, or copulation. They hear the echoes of that transcendent Heavenly music in great earthly music. We must blot out those traces.

Great music is dangerous also because it creates a silence around it in the soul. In that silence the Enemy can do terrible things. See to it that your patient never gets to hear or sing anything like "Let All Mortal Flesh Keep Silence". We've pretty much abolished silence in his world and in his soul, to prepare him for Hell's eternal noise.

Their world is getting more like Hell every year. The three S-words—silence, solitude and simplicity—are nearly extinct. Great music is one of the first sources and last bastions of all three in the soul; that's why we've spent such effort seducing their composers and, when some escaped our clutches, influencing those who determine what music is sung and what is not. When an original artist escapes us, he usually runs afoul of administrators. Mortals fancy most artists are in Hell, because they're such non-conformists, and most administrators in Heaven, because they're such conformists. Hah! Leave it to mortals to get it exactly backward.

What we have to fear most is not great music itself but its use in adoration. Of course, they can misuse great music too in many ways, e.g., by performance-idolatry, making the music opaque instead of transparent to the transcendent; or by sentimentalism and subjectivism, by wallowing in their own feelings. But equally, alas, they can use even bad music, or none, as occasions for adoration.

Here's a dilemma we have not yet solved: If we leave them alone, they produce great music, art, liturgy, beauty and happiness. If we corrupt them, we substitute suffering for happiness. But that gives them the opportunity for toughness and sanctity. Like all suffering, corrupted music can boomerang on us.

The suffering is real. Notice the expression on the faces of the non-singer at Mass: Half are enduring. They look as if they have to go to the bathroom. They stick it out, patiently, humbly, faithfully. It's disgusting! It's no fun for them, but unfortunately, it's no fun for us either when they're so loyal without emotional aids.

I sometimes wonder whether all our strategy isn't just a cruel game of the Enemy's, with us as the puppets on His string, the worms on His hook, doing His dirty work for Him, being used, toughening up His saints.

You will, of course, not quote me on this.

Your affectionate uncle,

Snakebite

9

ON LITURGICAL LANGUAGE

My dear Braintwister,

We need to discuss, at this point, our work in corrupting liturgical language. Lest you consider this an esoteric specialty, consider the following three facts:

First, all language, language as such, is sacred—like life, death, sex and music. Most mortals no longer understand the mysterious power of words or of their perversions.

Second, the words of the Enemy's written revelation are doubly sacred, and if we can in any way deflate and diminish their power, we blunt the very sword of the Spirit, and score a double victory: against language in general and against the most special and dangerous words in the world.

Third, words used liturgically become a form of music, and so all the things I wrote you about music in my last letter also apply to them.

Let's look at these three facts more carefully, so that you can understand Hell's general strategy and dovetail your individual work into it accordingly.

First, about the sacredness of language. Unfortunately, this is not totally forgotten. Some of their philosophers have let that old cat out of the bag, even agnostics like Heidegger. But who reads or understands him, anyway, except his own coterie of specialists? Yet there are dangerously illuminating passages like this one: "Words and language are not just labels for the commerce of those who write and speak. Rather, it is *in* words and language that things first come into being and are. It is for this reason that a misrelation to language, in the form of idle chatter or slogans, means a misrelation to being itself." He called language "the house of being". That old unbeliever knew better than most believers that "in the beginning was the Word".

Another agnostic among them, George Orwell, said something similar. In *1984,* the totalitarian government invents a new ongoing language, Newspeak, which keeps having fewer and fewer words in it, so that eventually, all undesirable concepts like freedom and self are removed from the language like tumors. The principle is simple but brilliant: *Logos* means three things—a word, the idea or concept expressed by the word, and the form or essence in reality known by the concept; and these three are so closely connected that a change in language results in a change in thought. When a word loses its meaning for humans, that aspect of reality does the same, for there are no longer any holding places for it in their mind. Without the right verbal cubbyhole, the letters from reality get lost.

That troublemaking reformer, Confucius, understood the importance of language. His social reforms ended China's seemingly endless wars and produced the longest, most stable social order (2,100 years) in history. His program's platform included only a few essential planks, and one of them he called "the restoration of names". He knew language structured thought and behavior as a riverbank structures the river's water.

But most modern mortals have forgotten that. And therein lies our strategic advantage. We concentrate much of our effort on this area of the battlefield, while they ignore it. And it's right near the center!

Second, the language of the Bible, which is also the basis for the language of their liturgy, must be doubly attacked because it's doubly powerful. Here are two parts to our strategy:

First, we play on Catholic suspicions of Protestant bib-liolatry—a suspicion that results in most Catholics having less of a Catholic, sacramental sense of sacredness when it comes to Scripture than Protestants do.

The second and more important part of our biblical strategy is to inspire translators to tamper with the text, by turning up their scholarly noses at the very idea of literal translation. The fussy little emendations seem harmless, but they establish the important principle that turns translating into interpreting and confuses translation with paraphrase. Once they accept the prin-ciple that the translator's business is not just to carry the mail but to edit it, our camel's nose is under their tent. The original text has become a nose of wax to be twisted at will; the receivers of revelation become the revisers of it, and thus the judges over it; and exegesis (reading-*out* meaning) becomes eisagesis (reading-*in* meaning). It may seem a modest beginning, but look what it's the beginning of: the denial of objective truth.

A third salient fact is that liturgical words are a form of music. So we've made those words as unmusical as possible, both in the Bible and in the liturgy. That takes half their power away.

The effect of the old, musical, poetic words in Scripture and liturgy was often terrible to us. Their musical character made them memorable, and memory made them musical. These two things reinforce each other.

Until recently, nearly everyone was familiar with the words of Scripture. When they had only two English translations of the Bible, the Douay and the King James, they all knew thousands of memorable, musical quotations. Now that there are dozens of translations, no one remembers the words any more, and we've wiped the music from their minds.

They say (the fools!) that "familiarity breeds contempt". In fact, of course, it's exactly the opposite: It's familiarity that breeds affection. That's why the Hebrew poets used parallelism:

if you say a thing twice, it sinks in, like two anchors or two nails instead of one. If you sing the same song a hundred times, you never forget it.

Ah, but we've abolished both the memory and the music, both the familiarity of the old words and the musical character of the new words. The result of the confusing plethora of new, unpoetic translations is simply that the words become forgettable, and therefore they are forgotten. It's like locking the door to an arsenal: Some of their most powerful weapons against us are just no longer available to them.

What was so powerful about the old words? Well, the old translations combined two things the new ones usually don't: clarity and profundity, simplicity and awesomeness, lowliness and height. The translation that American Catholics have had forced down their throats at Mass for the last decade or two was actually overseen by bishops, of all people! American bishops are far more like businessmen than like poets. A bishop-generated Bible is almost like a computer-generated love poem.

The result was a triumph of Hellspeak: modern, flat, pedestrian language that never sounds like a trumpet and usually sounds like a business memo. We've squashed all the spires and ground everything into oatmeal. Every striking, poetic word or image was deliberately toned down, lest anyone be awakened or moved.

Most of the parishioners now think the original text of the Bible is like that, and that the poetic style of the old translations was added by the old translators. They don't know the secret that the original is terribly poetic, and the poetry was subtracted by the new translators, not added by the old. They'd discover that if they knew Greek or Hebrew, but only scholars study that any more, and they're the easiest of all to hoodwink, because they so often put their hearts on hold.

The effect on the liturgy was predictable. First, no one listens to the readings—who listens to a business memo unless he has to? Second, if someone does, the reaction is a yawn and an "of course" rather than a sense of mystery, a sense of depth, a sense that there's anything more there to understand and to sink into or swim around in, a sense that the revealed mind of the Enemy just might exceed what they knew already.

Remember the power of boredom! Lately we've caught many more souls through boredom than through heresy or outright rebellion. We no longer bother tempting many to direct heresy. For one thing, it tends to cultivate the unfortunate habit of honest truth-seeking. For another thing, once there's that caring and passion and movement in a soul, it's perilously easy for the Enemy to change the direction of the movement. It's easier to move a car in the right direction if it's already moving, even if it's moving in the wrong direction, than it is to start a car moving when it's stuck. We can't overdo temptations to sloth today; you can't have too much nothingness.

One of the reasons we're spending so much effort thwarting the Catholic reunion with Anglicans is because Catholics might then use the Book of Common Prayer (with modest revisions), and that's the most dangerous thing in the English language since the King James Bible.

We've also spent enormous effort fostering an irrational fear of Latin and the Latin Mass on the part of local bishops and pastors. Both the Pope and the people love it and want it, of course, but the middle management treats it like the plague. Some pastors fear it as an alien intruder to their new up-to-date religion (it is).

How did we ever succeed in that con job? Ideology, Braintwister, ideology: one of Hell's greatest inventions. We've ideologized language. The reason they fear the Latin Mass is because we've associated it in their minds with right-wing extremists. I know this makes as much logical sense as identifying the American flag with the John Birch Society or the Ku Klux Klan, but once they believe in ideology they no longer believe in logic.

And then there is the feminists' demand to abolish the generic "he" and "mankind", which they consider "sexist". The feminists won't stop there, of course (especially not if we keep hot on their heels). They insist they be given the right to correct the Enemy Himself and rename Him "Her" or "It"! And the bishops often fear the feminists more than they fear the Enemy Himself.

We're not through, by any means. You would not believe our plans for future translations and mutilations. Wait till you see our planned "Lifestyles Interfacing" version! Literal versions will soon be as rare as literal virgins.

If only we could extend our future plans into the past and change history! Just imagine—if the Enemy had consulted a conference of bishops in creating the world, or inspiring the prophets! In America a bishop equals an administrator, and prophet and poet are two things no administrator is. The chief bishop in Rome, inconveniently, is both. And so are all the saints.

We can't abolish either of those two qualities from any of the saints, however diverse a lot they are. Poetry and prophecy are to be found in the simple language of Mother Teresa and the complex language of Cardinal Newman; in the acerbic acid of Amos and Jerome and in the surpassing sweetness of Isaiah and Bernard of Clairvaux. I'm afraid all the saints are poets, just because the Enemy is a poet (He invented things like babies and daisies and stars and worms and hurricanes.) The closer they get to Him, the closer they get to all His attributes.

Alas, their innate love of beauty, even in language, can't be permanently or totally eradicated from their souls in this world. But we can at least make them feel guilty and "elitist" about it:

How dare they build Gothic cathedrals in words today? Who do they think they are, anyway? — better than ordinary people, with ordinary words?

Vatican II put Scripture back on a pedestal, both private and public, both devotional and liturgical. So we had to arrange for most Catholic colleges to interpret this as a go-ahead for destructive scholarship, not for edifying common use. One of our greatest triumphs of the century was in Catholic theology departments: The very agencies supposed to carry out the Council's restoration of Scripture now routinely undermine it, and thus weaken the foundations of the faith of millions of students. We even got them to call their demythologizing away all the miracles "higher criticism"! What would "lower criticism" possibly be? They'll find out!

That arch-troublemaker, Archbishop Fulton Sheen, saw through our strategy. Shortly before he died, he advised Catholic parents who wanted to be sure their children did lose their faith to send them to Catholic colleges and be sure they took lots of theology courses.

Besides undermining their faith, we've also given them the impression that the world's most popular book could be understood only by professional scholars (in fact, they're the only ones in the world who can misunderstand it that badly!); that the world's most exciting book is the dullest book in the world, and that the millions who fed at that table for millennia were simply superstitious simpletons mumbling misunderstood formulas for their private fantasies.

Fortunately for us, Christendom is now so well divided that they'll never get together on one standard translation again. We keep them moving, and inspire new translations every year: the Liturgical Fidget must be supplemented by the Biblical Fidget. After all, the Bible has to keep up with the "progress" of the language (i.e., the decay of words).

Once, in King James' day, Scripture led the English language. Now, it follows it—to the dump, just as the American Church is following the world to the dump rather than leading it to the Heavens. Their "dumpster language" is an index of their dumpster destination. Keep giving your patient little pushes in that direction, and he'll ride with increasing speed the bandwagon of Our Father Below down to the place of pure noise (with lyrics of perfect torment).

Your affectionate uncle,

Snakebite

HOW TO SABOTAGE WORSHIP

My dear Braintwister,

A final few words on how to distract your patient from worship if you can't persuade him to stay away from church altogether.

You know, it's possible to persuade some Catholics as well as Protestants that liturgy is the least important of the three divisions of religion. The three things every religion has are creed, code and cult; or, words, works and worship; or theology, morality and liturgy. We can often convince almost anyone except the Eastern Orthodox of two lies: first, to separate the three parts in their mind, and second, to demote the third one to third place, as an extra, a mere "expression" of something more "spiritual", or even as "merely ceremonial". Intellectuals, especially, are often prone to that suggestion.

On the other hand, it's also possible to convince many, especially "cafeteria Catholics", that this is the only important area and that doctrine and morality are merely disposable excess baggage. Both useful errors stem from the common source-lie of separating the three areas. It's always in our interest to foster separations, oppositions, rivalries. It's also in our interest to foster confusions. What we hate is a clear structure, a one-in-many, like a body, or a building, or a *Summa*.

The obvious angle from which to insert opposition into the liturgy is that of the vertical vs. the horizontal, the sacred vs.

the secular. If you can only ideologize your patient into either a leftist or a rightist, he'll then think of Church as either simply "community" or simply "adoration" but never as communal adoration. Keep his attention and imagination off the Cross: It's a most troublesome, potent symbol of the joining, without the confusing, of the horizontal and the vertical.

Unfortunately, to know how to corrupt worship, we must first turn our attention to the painful subject of true worship according to the Enemy's plan. He instituted it for two reasons, an objective reason and a subjective one. First, for justice, for His verminous human slaves to give Him what He claims is objectively due to Him. That's the primal lie, of course, that Our Father Below exposed when he withdrew his support and set up our lowerarchy.

The second purpose of worship is psychological: to free humans from self-obsession and plunge them into self-forgetful adoration, appreciation, awe, love and joy—in other words, a rehearsal for Heaven. (Yes, Braintwister, all those scalding words have to be spoken.)

This state of soul that the Enemy designed worship to produce can be described in terms of an electroencephalogram. It's the state of strong alpha waves (i.e., awake, aware, alive) and weak beta waves (agitation, worry, selfish passion). We must keep them from that former state of mind because it is like that of the Enemy Himself.

How do we do it? By swinging their souls' pendulum between boredom and worry, between sloth and anxiety, between death and nightmares. In other words, we must stamp the psychic image of Hell on their stupid identities. Their only aliveness must be worry, and their only peace must be death.

When we deal with worship, we have a special difficulty with Catholics, who have that unique obscenity they call the Mass. All over the world, a thousand times every minute, the Enemy rubs our noses in our biggest defeat; for the Mass is the repeated celebration and actual representation of Our Father Below's one mistake, when he let the human race slip out of his fingers at the very moment that seemed to be his supreme triumph: when he killed the Enemy's Son. Rage, rage, rage . . .

Well. Now that we have composed ourselves like gentlemen . . . let us consider a practical topic: the use and misuse of material aids the mortals employ in their worship. They use them, surprisingly, not to gather things in to themselves, as they usually do with material things, like money and food, but precisely to transcend themselves and get their minds "into" the Enemy's mind and will, by focusing on a crucifix or a statue or the tabernacle.

Now, we can pervert their use of material things in worship in either of two ways: idolatry or pride. Idolatry turns these means into ends. It makes them things that are opaque, like walls. Unfortunately, this can't be done with one material thing, the Host, because that actually *is* the Enemy. But it's easy to get them to idolize other things, for they're animals, after all, and all their knowledge begins with sensation, so they find it hard to get the airplane of their souls up off that runway. We can shoot down most of their planes on the ground. But they keep trying, and their very efforts, though failures, often do us more harm than their successes. So this temptation has very limited use.

The second temptation, to pride, is better if we can manage it. We make them think they're "spiritual", and superior and that they don't really need all this vulgar, common, materialistic stuff. (We do this especially at Christmas time.) It's not easy to convince them of such an absurdity, but it's possible, and when successful, it pays the greatest dividends. Pride is the most delicious of sins to our palates.

The Enemy-designed goal of worship—pure, self-forgetful adoration of the Enemy for His own sake—is very hard for them, ever since Our Father's triumph in Eden. But it happens, especially at Mass, where it comes from their faith in the Real Presence of the Enemy's Son in the Sacrament. His whole mystical Body is present too, and they usually forget that, except for the Eastern Orthodox, who believe that each saint whose icon is present is also there.

This belief must be ruthlessly attacked, watered down, nuanced—whatever. Use every trick in the book. They'll fall for the lowest. You'll be amazed how easy it is to turn your patient's attention from his Creator to his neighbor's T-shirt or worries about his car or even a loose button! It's utterly hilarious how irrational they are. How the Enemy can pretend to love such animals as these, is a mystery Hell has never figured out. What's He really up to? It doesn't make sense. How could He really care about a creature so weak that a speck of dust on the pew looms larger than the greatest miracle in history made really present on the altar?

But don't get carried away with the fun and ease of distracting them. When they return their thoughts, by an act of will, away from our distractions and to the Enemy, that act of will is of greater power and value to the Enemy than the greatest emotional highs that come to them without their will, even the most "religious" highs. That's why He allows so many distractions and doesn't zap them away by His power: because those acts of will stem from and strengthen the central part of their souls, their real selves, the eternal things we lust to churn round in Hell's blenders and then devour. Everything else— *everything* —is a mere means to capturing that: the I, the image of the Enemy Himself.

The Enemy's command to worship includes a command for a Sabbath rest. Most mortals don't realize the importance of this commandment, and that fact has enabled us to get modern Christians to disobey this one more than any of the others (except the two on sex, obviously). The importance of the Sabbath command is their need for leisure.

They need leisure as much as they need work. So we've been at work abolishing leisure from their land, through all the time-saving devices of modern technology! After all, we have no leisure in Hell; why should those vermin have it on earth?

The Sabbath commandment to take leisure is the only commandment which is always an immediate joy for them to obey both outwardly and inwardly. It's like a "take five" from a conductor or a job foreman. So we've bent our backs to bend their noses to the grindstone. We've made their age "the Age of Anxiety". We've gotten them to the state where they simply can't comprehend the Enemy's Son's command to "be anxious for nothing". Anxiety is the very air they breathe; how could He tell them to hold their breath?

One of them once told the story of a farmer carrying a donkey on his back to market. A neighbor drove by in a wagon and told the farmer to come up on the wagon instead of carrying the donkey himself and breaking his back. So he climbed on the wagon; but when they got to market, the farmer's back was broken anyway, because he had never put the donkey down! That's the idiocy we can and must suck them into, even in church. Make them keep their burdens on their own backs even when they're on the Enemy's wagon.

Keep them at it incessantly. Don't let them trust the Enemy's promises and hand their burdens over to Him. Make them repeat slogans like "God helps those who help themselves", and "Fear God but keep your powder dry"—and make them forget the first half of each saying (just as we get many fundamentalists and charismatics to forget the second half). Make them so "realistic" and "practical" (really just the opposite, of course!) that they dismiss the Enemy's clear promises as vague, rhetorical exaggerations. Don't let them take their hands off the steering wheel of their own lives for a moment. No vacation, no Sabbath, no leisure, no rest, forever. Train them for the treadmills of Hell.

If you can't keep your patient's worries on himself, at least keep them on something, even his family. Of course, genuine concern for the family is very unpleasant for us. But even this can be perverted easily into worry and used to block that trusting happiness the Enemy wants.

That trusting and happy attitude does their families more Enemy-type "good" than anything their worries can ever accomplish, of course. But worry can blind them to that obvious fact. The danger of letting them off the worry-hook is especially crucial when it comes to children. When children see happy, confident parents, they too learn to trust and relax and become fertile soil for the Enemy's seeds. But when the children see worried and unhappy parents, they unconsciously learn the lesson that life is a problem to be resented, not a mystery to be explored. And their souls become hard, rocky ground, hard for the Enemy's seed to take root in.

Distractions from Confession presents a different problem than distractions from Mass. It's nearly impossible to distract them *in* the confessional, so we must distract them *from* it, keep them away. Terrible things happen in that little black box! Next to the tabernacle on the altar, that's the place we fear more than any other on earth.

We've kept many away by the influence of modern psychology and its dismissal of sin and guilt. We've gotten a lot of mileage out of their confusion between guilt and guilt feelings, and between peace and peaceful feelings. Once they reduce those two objective realities to subjective feelings, we've got them hooked. For they can easily exchange guilty feelings for peaceful feelings by other means than confession, and they will. But the only sure way to escape real guilt and attain real peace is through the repentance and forgiveness that the Enemy instituted. So we have to Dim the Lights: Don't let them make that distinction. In fact, don't let them think in plain, simple reasonable terms about any objective reality at all.

Confession and Communion are the closest they get to Heaven on earth. The power in the Host is greater than the power in an atom bomb. So if we keep them away from the sacraments, it's like persuading an enemy not to load his guns. There are places on earth where our success has been overwhelming. Do you know how many confessions were heard throughout one entire diocese in the Netherlands during one entire year recently? None!

Don't be deterred by the awful discomfort the Enemy's nearness causes when you approach the sacraments with your patient. For here is the very heart of the battlefield, where the Enemy Himself is present. He can be hurt there, at least vicariously, in His Body, His people. For fool that He is, He has made Himself really one with all those vermin that now make up His Body, like a maggot-heap. We can't hurt Him any longer—Our Father Below did that on Calvary—but we can hurt the ones He loves and has united Himself with. To get at Him there, even a little, is our only consolation, our drug. Anything for that end; that end justifies any means.

It's not fair, Braintwister, not fair—that those vermin can imbibe a miracle any time they want just by walking down the road, entering a building, and eating a thing that looks like bread. How vulgar of the Enemy to cast His pearls before swine! If only we could abolish those obscene sacraments! But whenever we try that, by inspiring tyrants like Stalin or Mao to persecute religious believers, it only strengthens the Church in the long run. The dead leaves drop off, the life of the plant goes underground, and it sprouts up again with martyrs as its flowers.

Just keep him away, Braintwister, keep him away.

Your affectionate uncle,

Snakebite

II

ON CATHOLIC EDUCATION

My naïve Braintwister,

Your last report to me both fills me with delight and appalls me with terror. The delight comes from a sterling opportunity to corrupt your patient's faith and morals that's just fallen into your lap; the horror comes from your obvious incomprehension of that opportunity.

So your patient has enrolled in a Catholic college: Don't you understand that this increases, not decreases, our opportunities?

Really, Braintwister, what do you do with all those tactical advisories we send you?

You see, our overall social strategy for decades now has been to attack the Church from within, with spiritual spies and fifth columnists, not from without. The simple, direct attack from without by persecution—physical or verbal—never really worked well in the long run, though it gave us a lot of pleasure in the short run. In ancient Rome, persecutions eventually helped convert half the world to our Enemy in only three centuries. Their cliché about the blood of the martyrs being the seed of the Church proved quite true, alas.

Look at modern China for example. After 50 years of doors open to Western missionaries, there were only 2 million Christians in China. But after 30 years of Mao Tse-Tung's very thoroughgoing persecutions, there were 20 million of those vermin! The persecutions that we instigated to divide their numbers actually multiplied them.

And not only the quantity but also the quality. Compare the disgusting spiritual state of the Church in countries where we've arranged for juicy persecutions (the communist countries before the fall of communism)—Russia, Poland, East Germany—with the wonderfully weak, faddish compromises in the Church in countries where we've used the new strategy—Holland, England, America, West Germany.

We've finally had the realism to admit that the old strategy worked only to give us temporary kicks, not long term success. The gates of the Church only got stronger when Hell's battering ram hit them from outside. But they got weaker when we wormed our way inside and ate at the door like termites.

This is especially true of Catholic schools. And education is the key to power in modern society. The university is far more powerful than the government. It molds men's minds. And it's answerable to no electorate.

Just look at what we've done in one short generation to Catholic schools. Back in the '50s, when Catholic parents sent their kids to Catholic schools, they could at least trust them to teach whatever the Enemy had revealed. Of course, they couldn't guarantee that the lessons would "take", because of the Enemy's own stupid and self-defeating invention of human free will. But they could at least count on the school helping their cause, not undermining it.

Now, it's almost exactly the opposite. The strongest Catholics are frequently the converts, or the ones who went to non-Catholic schools. Meanwhile, the Catholic schools are a veritable feast for us. Instead of believing more, and more strongly when they exit than when they enter, the typical kid believes less, and less strongly after than before. What wonderful irony!—as if a patient would go to the hospital to get sick, not to get well.

Just contemplate this picture for a moment, Braintwister—a very common and realistic picture indeed—and you'll start salivating with delight. Millions of innocent, naïve, hard-working parents scrape together big bucks for tuition money for Catholic high schools and colleges—usually a heroic, sometimes nearly miraculous task for middle-class parents nowadays. They put themselves in debt sometimes for life. For what? For their precious kiddies' welfare, academic and spiritual.

And it usually does pay off academically, at both religious and secular private schools. Although even there, this is the first generation of Americans who know less than their parents.

Let's look at secular private schools first. There, all the social problems that we've foisted on their society are magnified. Four out of five kids there come from broken homes and feel dumped. Most of them do drugs. Nearly all do America's favorite drug, alcohol. Virgins are about as common as unicorns. And they're nearly all hurting inside, and cynical outside.

And Catholic schools are increasingly similar. As our attack on the family expands throughout their society, Catholic families now look absolutely indistinguishable from unbelieving families: They have only a few kids, they worry about money, they think responsibility is consumerism, they practice and justify fornication, divorce, abortion, contraception—the whole package deal. So the typical Catholic school student is now indistinguishable from the non-Catholic.

Except for one thing: the opportunity for hypocrisy. They're expected to play the Catholic game, to believe the old orthodoxies, but as often as not, they don't. They sometimes even learn that little two-step from their religion teachers. We've gotten it to the point now where the theology professor in a Catholic college who believes what the Church believes is the rare exception, not the rule, and is often made to feel like a fanatic and a menace. Yet these unbelievers call themselves Catholics. Students catch on to this trick of rubber words very quickly.

It's even more delicious for us in the practical, moral area, because that's where the rubber meets the road. Most administrators and public relations people who try to sell Catholic schools to Catholic parents today try to justify calling their school "Catholic", even when they've abandoned Catholic dogmas, because it teaches "Catholic values". Values is our nice, new, "soft" term for subjective morality. Practical parents are usually most concerned with morality. But the "advanced" morality that's taught is full of the same "advanced" decay that's turning their social body into a corpse.

Especially, the morality that's taught by example. Sometimes the typical dormitory at the typical Catholic college in America on the typical weekend can make ancient Rome look positively Puritan. Half the students are drunk out of their minds any given Friday or Saturday night. Many of them are fornicating, without the slightest question or qualm of conscience. Their teachers just don't talk about this because they don't dare tell them anything unpopular anymore, especially about their sex lives. Meanwhile, they feel self-righteous and non-conformist by protesting racism, militarism and other evils they're not really in any danger of.

We're still working to extend this spectacular sexual success to other areas of morality. But fear not, Braintwister, it will follow, as night follows day. The Enemy's morality is a seamless whole. You can't unravel one main thread of His garment without eventually pulling the whole thing loose, especially when the thread is as close to the center and source of life as sex is. Remember, we've already got them desensitized to murdering their own unborn babies. The right to fornicate leads to the right to murder. If we can do *that,* we can do anything.

Of course, if parents had any idea of the magnitude of what actually goes on in the classrooms and the dorm rooms, enrollments and tuition monies would dry up and Catholic education would go out of business. So the administration has only three choices: to cover up, to crack down, or to pack up shop. They're too afraid to crack down or to pack up, so they do the easy thing; they cover up.

You see, it's the old bargain with Faust updated. As their society has upped the price of a college education in dollars, we've done it in souls. We sell an education in apostasy and they pay for it by giving up their faith, the honest search for objective truth, belief in objective values, the authority of the Church, their virginity and their society.

Best of all, we teach them that a little hypocrisy goes a long way. We learned that in Germany during the war. The German people knew about the concentration camps, all right, but they pretended not to, with the rationalization, "What can we do about it, anyway?" Their educators have the same mindset; even their pastors. "They're going to do it anyway, so what can we do?" is their excuse for changing the moral lessons to fit the lifestyles of the students, rather than vice versa. Can you imagine the Enemy's Son ever thinking that way? Apparently they can!

We're rapidly replacing reason with rationalization. The students learn little shuffling word-games from their teachers, especially in theology. They learn to call apostasy "dissent", heresy "nuancing", baby-killing "choice", sodomy an "alternative lifestyle", and adultery "adult". Their verbal hypocrisy rationalizes their lived hypocrisy. They learn how simultaneously to live decadence and to talk idealism, especially about faraway things they can do nothing about, like South Africa and El Salvador, and nonthreatening fashionable causes like recycling and saving endangered species. So they really believe they're all "good people". They simply don't believe in sin anymore (or, of course, in us). That means no more guilt for us to feast on. But instead, something even better: not hurting souls but sleeping and dying souls.

The orthodox who speak out against this are ineffective because they preach only to the converted. Liberals and conservatives never read each other's writings. Also, most of them are pretty shallow, because even the conservatives usually argue and worry about doctrinal and moral heresies and ignore our deepest work of all, the beginnings of that mental habit of hypocrisy, pretense, or the divided soul. Some day, we hope, it will be so divided that its name will be "Legion" eternally.

And you're complaining that your patient has stepped into this trap of ours by enrolling in a Catholic college! See how "out of it" you are?

Unfortunately, we haven't yet worked this strategy with equal success on all Catholic colleges; and many of the high schools are still quite backward and traditional. But even there, though the high schools aren't quite so desperate to be avant garde as the colleges are, we use intellectual fashion and prestige to hook our academic fish: a more modest, in-house prestige. Teachers who want to be "liked" by students let the students think and do pretty much what they please. You see, those Americans are absolutely terrified of not being "accepted". If the prophets had been Americanized like that, there would have been no prophets.

I notice further that your patient has enrolled in a Jesuit college; how fortunate! The Jesuits used to be our worst enemies, the Pope's shock troops. How times have changed! There are still some formidable spiritual warriors for the Enemy there, but the most advanced dissenters are there too, those who sneer at the Pope, often openly. Your job now is to see to it that your patient is taught by that kind of "bold" thinker (really a worm and a Quisling, of course).

Always remember, a sneer is more potent than any argument. Any substitute for reason is our ally, but the sneer is doubly effective because it adds arrogance.

Unfortunately, the Enemy spoke the truth when He promised them that all real seekers find. So keep him from seeking. The best way is to get him believing he's seeking truth when he's really seeking acceptance. If you finally succeed in putting out that fire of real doubt and questioning in his soul, we'll have some delicious devil's food to feed on forever at the banquet table of Our Father Below.

That's what it's all about, of course, the Bottom Line. That's what everything is for in our work, just as everything the Enemy commands is for the opposite end. But how many of them are even taught that simplest and most primary of all practical truths anymore?

Your affectionate uncle,

Snakebite

12

ON ELITISM AND EGALITARIANISM
IN CATHOLIC EDUCATION

My dear Braintwister,

I see that your patient's theology professor is just the kind of person we want for the job: an ex-priest who left the Church and became some kind of Marxist in the '6os, then apparently returned to the fold. But he's brought along some key concepts we can get a lot of mileage out of, especially his adamant egalitarianism.

Of course the Catholic religion isn't egalitarian; how could a universe created and ruled by the Enemy be equal to its Creator? How could the human vermin, created in the Enemy's image, be equal to the beasts? How could every thought and feeling in their souls be of equal value? But never let him ask such simple questions as that.

Professor Fenster's thoughts are an orgy of "openness". His re-found Catholicism is a matter of moral sentiment, not dogma. In fact, his mind is mush. Unfortunately, his heart is genuinely good and caring and loving. He'd willingly die for his neighbor (but not for God, who remains far away and shadowy to him). But fortunately, we can use his very virtues against him, especially his sense of compassion and his hatred of snobbery. Of course this is a principle of the Enemy, and we can't distort the principle itself, but we can distort the way he understands and applies it.

You see, he's so ideological about his egalitarianism that Fogpipe, the tempter we've assigned to him, has had no trouble at all getting him to look at everyone who doesn't share his egalitarian tastes as an "elitist", an "authoritarian", "oppressive", and even a "fascist". (Those words have no real cognitive meaning in his mind, of course; they merely express feelings, not facts.) Thus, in the very name of egalitarianism, he has become a snob!

We can easily make him play the part of the pharisee at the very time he thinks he's playing the publican. For the real pharisee today is just the opposite from what he was in the Enemy's day. The heretics call the orthodox "pharisaical" today, just because they're faithful to the old orthodoxy. Thus they pray, in effect, "Thank you, Lord, that I am not like that pharisee!" Thus we get them to confuse fidelity with hypocrisy, in fact to call the honest love of truth a form of dishonesty!

We could never manipulate the old, instinctive, populist egalitarianism that way. We couldn't sneak in to the old minds through that opening wedge of modern ideology, the wonderful habit of looking at ideas first and reality second. The old, realistic populism simply followed the Enemy's ridiculous attraction for poor, ordinary people—a habit the saints picked up from the Enemy without Fenster's ideological baggage.

The Enemy wants them to be discriminating and critical and "elitist" about ideas, and open and tolerant and egalitarian about people. So we must get them to be exactly the opposite: egalitarian about ideas and elitist about people. Instead of loving sinners and hating sin, we must get them to love sins and hate sinners—or better, hate saints. Instead of loving heretics and hating heresies, we must get them to love heresies and hate heretics—or better, hate the faithful or at least scorn them and feel superior to them.

If we can't do that, at least we can confuse the two together, so they'll either love the heresy along with the heretic (the liberal temptation) or hate the heretic along with the heresy (the conservative temptation). In the past, it was easier to get them to hate heretics and harder to get them to love heresies. Today, it's the opposite. Who cares which road they take, as long as it's not the Enemy's?

What's most fun of all for us is to move them from an initial egalitarianism of people (like Fenster's) to an egalitarianism of ideas (Fenster's already there), and then to an elitism and snobbery against those people whose ideas are not as egalitarian as theirs. Thus we get them to think that they're being tolerant at the very time they're being intolerant.

Until you've been at it as long as I have, you simply won't believe how easy it is to dupe them with words, Braintwister— even the educated ones, who study propaganda techniques and logical fallacies; in fact, they're the easiest to con. We've gotten many of them to be dogmatically anti-dogmatic and snobbishly anti-snobbish.

Fenster thinks he's on a righteous crusade for "democracy" in the Church. So whenever the Pope says something authoritative, he comes out with a snide remark about "despotism" and "patriarchy". Not arguments, of course, but innuendo. Since certain words are emotional knee-jerks for him, he uses them as little hammers on his students' minds, and eventually they learn to jerk their mental knees in sync.

It can't be repeated too often, Braintwister: Never try to use reason to tempt them. Reason is our enemy. Get them to think of reason itself as unfeeling, or old-fashioned, or even Eurocentric.

It hardly matters what's substituted for reason's thirst for truth. Even things like justice and compassion can work, because divorced from truth, they become something other than true justice or true compassion. If they can be led to put political relevance or utility in the place of truth as their standard and ideal, they're in our net, ready to be manipulated.

Fenster still likes to quote Karl Marx's saying, "Philosophers have only interpreted the world; the thing is to change it." That's close to the saying of that unsubtle Marxist, Mao Tse-Tung: "Ideas are not pictures but bullets. What's important is not their theoretical conformity to some pre-existing reality, but their power to create a new reality." In other words, serve power, not truth. The very philosophy of Hell—today they call it Deconstructionism.

Unlike Marx and Mao, Fenster is a moralist with a Catholic veneer. I won't call him a "Catholic" moralist, because his morality amounts to little more than: It's nice to be nice. But it's enough to appeal to your patient's moral feeling for justice, peace and compassion. Then, after many classes with this nice man, the feeling begins to rub off that there's something self-contradictory in the Catholic religion; that the moral ideal is soft, loving, and open, but the theology is hard, nasty and oppressive. It's sheer nonsense, of course. The Enemy wants them to have hard heads and soft hearts, and there's no more contradiction in that than in having hard fingernails and soft fingers. But if you repeat nonsense enough times to them, in different words, in masked and indirect forms, they'll eventually come to think there's something to it.

Case in point: Fenster already has your patient sympathizing with those little grandstanders whom the Vatican has dared to label unorthodox. Though your student patient still believes the orthodox doctrines, he already feels more sympathy for the labeled heretics than for the labeling Church. In fact, he's feeling bad vibes toward the very word "labeling". In other words, he's learning to scorn truth. What a wedge that is!

We accomplished that partly through the negative emotions he associates with the word "censorship" as something inherently "oppressive" and "elitist". Of course, this is nonsense rationally. To promote health, you must censor disease. To promote accuracy, you must censor inaccuracy. Every doctor, scientist and mathematician does that. But we must use words like bullets, not like pictures, just as Mao said: to kill thought, not to nourish it.

Though your patient is quite bright, he has not noticed the self-contradiction in Fenster's attack on Rome's "censorship" of the heretical theologians. The Pope, of course, doesn't want to take away the heretics' freedom to speak; he only claims the right to label their thoughts as "not what the Catholic Church teaches". But Fenster wants to take away the Pope's freedom to say that. So Fenster and his ilk really want to censor the Pope more than the Pope wants to censor them.

Be careful: Don't let your patient get anywhere near that simple thought. Keep him away from the habit of simple thought. Above all, don't let him discover Chesterton. That arch-troublemaker let thousands of our cats out of the bag. Let him meet a few "traditionalist" Catholics of the angry, "gloom and doom" type, so that he comes to think all the orthodox are like that; and be sure he meets only likable heretics like Fenster, so he comes to love the heresies through loving the heretics. Don't ever let him meet anyone like Mother Teresa; that would absolutely shatter the categories.

Also, don't let him read De Tocqueville. That busybody understood Americans better than any American ever did. He understood that Americans are conformists who think of themselves as nonconformists. This is especially true of the young, who have to nonconform to forge their individual identity but still feel insecure enough to need peer group approval desperately. The whole country takes its cue from its youth. The little coteries of scholars are like teen-agers, echoing their in-group orthodoxies, which are their avant-garde attacks on popular tradition.

As pre-teens, Americans learn the fun of shocking the "old folks". Later, it becomes the serious "create your own values" stage—as if values belonged to individuals like material possessions. Next, they can be made to hate or fear standards themselves as "oppressive" and to want to lower all standards to a common level. The easiest ways to do this are relativism and subjectivism. If anything goes, anyone can qualify.

You can probably make a strong connection in his unconscious between educational standards and religious standards, and you can get him to lower either one by getting him to lower the other. Cheap thoughts and cheap grace are sold in the same spiritual junk store: ours.

Speaking of educational standards, I'm thrilled to see that Fenster hates the "Great Books" people and their philosophy, their curricula and their colleges. In fact, he hates the very word "great", the very concept of greatness, excellence, or superiority. Once we get them to scorn both the past (out of which the Great Books come) and standards of excellence, we can teach them great gobs of ignorance about their history (e.g., calling the Middle Ages the "Dark Ages"). Some of their most widely used history books are already full of outright lies.

Your patient being at a Catholic college gives us many advantages. At a secular college, Catholics know they're distinctive *qua* Catholic. But at a big Catholic college, they have to be distinctive by being different from the Catholic mainstream, which they think their school represents.

Ironically, at very secular colleges, such as the Ivy League, there are often strong groups of Catholic students. They have to put on intellectual muscle. They're strong because they're waging a spiritual and intellectual war, and they know it. Few of them know that at Catholic colleges anymore. All they teach is peace, peace, when there is no peace.

Keep at it, Braintwister, and your patience will be rewarded in your patients. Fogpipe will keep at Fenster and be sure no light comes through that window. Just be sure your patient doesn't discover Chesterton or Lewis or Muggeridge. Get set for that long haul, for propaganda takes years to carve its ruts into the soul. But in the end, the ruts become dark and deep enough for us to slither right through them to dinner.

Your affectionate uncle,

Snakebite

13

ON WHAT THEY LEARN IN THEOLOGY CLASS

My dear Braintwister,

I see that your patient has enrolled in Professor Avant Garde's theology class. Wonderful news. You're finally catching on.

The best opportunities of all come in theology classes. What a fabulous irony!—the very thing they think makes them distinctively Catholic, the very first thing parents think of when they consider sending their kids to a "Catholic" school, is the place where we've been able to undermine students' faith the most.

You see, we've managed to sneak what's virtually a whole new religion in under the all-purpose slogan of "the spirit of Vatican II". When they hear that phrase, they often just stop thinking, and a warm fuzzy comes over them. They conveniently forget to read the actual documents of Vatican II, and invoke its "spirit" to justify orgies of "openness"—openness to anything at all.

When I say it's often a whole new religion, I'm not exaggerating. The two fundamental categories of the old religion were sin and salvation. Every *Christian* thinker—Paul, Augustine, Aquinas, Luther, Calvin, Pascal, Newman, Kierkegaard, C. S. Lewis—these two themes. Subtract those two categories and it doesn't matter what you put in their place, you've got another religion. And the scholars' itch for change, novelty and fashion keeps them at "the theological fidget", ever new substitutes for the old basics: feminism, "New Age", "creation spirituality", "liberation theology", pop psychology, whatever.

The wedge we used to insert the new religion into the old one was the same trick we used so successfully 15–20 centuries ago: Gnosticism. We got them to exaggerate the distinction between the spirit and the letter so much that the new "spirit" flatly contradicts the old "letter" of the law. They're so confused they don't even think the obvious thought that the "spirit" has to be the spirit *of* the letter!

You'd think they'd learn from their past brush with Gnosticism. But, no, they neither know nor care about the past. You'd be amazed how many hoary old heresies we can refurbish and dress up as the latest novelty. The current Gnosticism is even more delightful to us than the old, because of the irony that the very people who scorn the letter, the concrete, the particular and the embodied, visible Church, are the very people that use "incarnational" as a favorite adjective. (It usually means to them just "worldly".) It's simply amazing, the contradictions and mental contortions they can be made to swallow, especially the scholars, whose feet long ago left the ground of common sense.

Their scholars and teachers, of course, know very well the contradiction between "the spirit of Vatican II" and the letter of its documents. They know that those documents reaffirmed the very things they despise: old things like the Latin Mass, the rosary, devotion to Mary, papal infallibility, traditional morality and the need to conform one's conscience to the teaching authority of the Church. But the students rarely read the documents, so they can be easily fooled.

Professor Garde is perfect for your purposes. He's a "reinterpreter" and a "nuancer". Your patient, all bright-eyed and bushy-tailed about his new faith, would recoil in horror if any of the old dogmas he has come to believe in were explicitly denied. But if they're "carefully nuanced" and "creatively reinterpreted", this can seem like a progress and a deepening at the very time it is really an emptying out of the substance.

What substance? Here are eight things Professor Garde will never mention if he can help it. Drop them out—drop any one of them out—and you have another religion. Garde will never deny them, of course; but anyone can see his mind is not formed by them. It breathes a different air.

First, the supernatural, especially miracles, especially the bodily resurrection of the Enemy's Son. Professor Garde says the Resurrection really happened, but "in the hearts of the disciples, not in the molecules of a corpse". This sounds so profound, so nice. Of course, what it really means is that we have no more to fear from that "myth" than from Santa Claus!

If Professor Garde has to mention the supernatural at all, he speaks of it as a "dimension of experience", not as an objective reality. This is much more effective than the old honest atheist-materialist arguments against miracles, which could be met and refuted on their own rational grounds.

Second, the divinity of the Enemy's Son. This is so "nuanced" and hedged around with technical terms that it becomes mean-ingless and incomprehensible. Once again, this is much more effective than outright denial, for that might move students onto the dangerous ground of giving reasons and searching for truth. We never let them get that far; we fudge the meanings.

Third, the worship and adoration of this dangerously con-crete object, the Enemy's Son. Deny the divinity and you dry up the worship. What's left is a vague, humanitarian admira-tion for the Son and a remote, deistic worship of the Enemy at a distance. We can't undo the Incarnation in fact, but we can undo it in their spiritual life. That's why we need to under-mine all the dogmas: They all make a difference not just to thought but to life, especially to the life of worship, that act that causes us such staggering pain whenever we are forced to behold it.

Fourth, the old idea of sacrifice, of a willing death to self. This is now scorned as bad old psychology, as repressive, self-loathing and unhealthy. Imagine—the thing that is the very life of the Enemy! Add to that this irony: they hold this new idea of self-caressing "self-affirmation" on the authority of the Enemy's Son Himself, now reinterpreted by His so-called followers.

Fifth, the idea of sin as something they are personally, individually guilty of and need to repent of and turn away from before they can be forgiven—this is seen as unfeeling, inhuman and lacking in "compassion". Consequently, that terrible place, the confessional, is used far, far less than it used to be.

Many of the young never go to confession. Many don't even know they're supposed to. What the Mass means without the concept of sin is a very different thing, of course, from what it really is. For without sin they don't need either a sacrifice or a Savior.

Sixth, we've taught them to scorn the authority of the Church and to sneer at the very idea of authority as "medieval" and "undemocratic". Their real religion is democracy, which means in their minds "freedom", which in turn usually means simply doing whatever they like.

Seventh, we've taken the spine out of morality. There are no longer any moral "laws", only "values" and "guidelines". Nothing is etched in stone, not even the Ten Commandments. Most campus ministers and theology teachers have simply given up in the area of sexual morality. Their attitude is: Nobody's going to obey anyway, so why command? Why be laughed at?

So they're either silent or they find ways to rationalize and compromise with the "sexual revolution". For instance, it's not fornication that's wrong any more, but not "respecting" or "loving" each other, or "treating each other as objects". They're too stupid to see that if copulation is justified by tender feelings, rather than by marriage, then the corollary is that many acts of married love after the honeymoon are sinful. If feeling in love justifies sex, then not feeling in love disqualifies it. In that case, many of them are illegitimate children!

Eighth, their prayer life disappears. In the new religion, self-manipulative "meditation exercises" take the place of prayer. Rare indeed is the Catholic college student who spends more than a minute a day in prayer. This means we've gotten them to stop shooting at us! Now we can shoot at them so much more easily.

But, you may wonder, how can this be? Their New Testament clearly teaches all eight of these things. How can they abandon them and still think of themselves as Christians?

The answer is in the mileage we've gotten out of the use (or abuse) of the historical-critical method of interpreting the New Testament. The "bottom line" result is that they no longer have any confidence that they know what the Enemy's Son actually said and did. Everything is "interpretation", nothing is data. It's like a rock turning into a marshmallow.

Just imagine the effect on the mind of your patient when the world-renowned scholar Avant Garde assures him that the words he found so powerful and precious didn't come from the Enemy's Son at all, but from the mythmaking, storytelling minds of "early Christian communities"—words like "I Am Who Am", and "I am the Way, the Truth and the Life; no one comes to the Father but through Me", and "This is My Body", and "You are Peter and on this rock I will build My Church". It's like all their cannonballs turning to rubber!

Most delicious of all is this irony: students accept Professor Garde's attack on the authority of the Church on the authority of the professor! After all, he knows so much more than they do. Of course, if they actually did think for themselves, as he preaches they should, they'd start to see through his unspoken assumptions and notice the strength of the old positions he ridicules. But it's so much easier to feel than to think, especially when you feel "in" or "with it".

Believe it or not, the strongest motive we've been able to use to corrupt the scholars, next to scholarly vanity and pride, has been sex. This trick is almost never uncovered among them. Only "extremists" say it, and no one believes them. Let me explain it to you.

The Enemy's Church teaches two things: dogma and ethics; and it's the ethics that touches people's lives most immediately. Now of all the parts of the Enemy's ethics, their society has abandoned His sexual ethic most completely. So someone who wants to be "modern" and justify his own sexual sins, will have a strong vested interest in any theory that weakens the authority of both the Church and the New Testament, both of which teach the hard, old, unpopular ethic of chastity.

There's even an unconscious connection between the new theories of the Resurrection and the new sex ethic. If the Enemy's Son didn't literally rise from the dead, then He can be only a man, not divine; and then His authority is not absolute and infallible. And then the Church He founded is no more infallible than its founder. So they don't have to take its sex ethic literally.

Of course, no one says this or even consciously thinks this connection. But it's there, unconsciously. They know of the existence of the unconscious, but they hardly suspect the connections and pathways there that we travel on.

Above all, insinuate rather than argue with your patient. As soon as you have to use reason, the light hurts you. Never forget Lesson One: Dim the Lights! Appeal to his desires, especially the desire to be "in", to be modern, and to justify instead of repenting his sins. Repentance is so un-progressive! If you succeed, the fun you have now will be nothing compared with the fun you'll have at the table of Our Father Below.

Your affectionate uncle,

Snakebite

14

ON DISINTEGRATION
AND INTEGRATION IN THEOLOGY

You idiot,

Now you've done it. In letting your patient become impatient with both his theology teachers, that brilliant heretic Avant Garde and that master of sweet dullness Fenster, you let him wander into a class taught by that simpleton, Father Heerema.

Didn't you read your scouting report on Heerema? He isn't famous, hasn't published any books and doesn't have a "dynamic personality"—but he's the most dangerous person in that whole theology department, because he has such a strong and clear grasp of the center, the hub that holds all the spokes of the wheel together; and your patient is on the verge of finding just that missing piece to the puzzle of his life.

Let me explain how crucial this is. For many centuries, we've been working on disintegrating their lives. This is the earthly preparation for that final disintegration of personality that we look forward to in Hell: feasting on souls torn into bite-sized little pieces. Now, the most effective means we have ever found to that end, next to the divided will, is the divided mind. This is especially true of the theological mind.

What divisions? I mentioned a few in my last letters, e.g., between the "spirit" and the "letter" of Vatican II, and of the Bible as well; and between their apparent egalitarianism and their real elitism, their apparent publicanism and real phariseeism. In addition to these divisions, there are, of course, the ever-popular denominational and ideological squabbles. But in this century especially, we've also been able to use a feature of their age, over-specialization, to make big rips seem to appear in the "seamless garment" of the Enemy's teaching. This works especially well in academic theology departments because most of the professors very much want to be accepted by the super-specialized scholarly establishment.

They're aware of the problem, but even those who bemoan specialization are ineffective in doing much about it, because most of them no longer have a clear vision of the center, the "one thing needful". If they think there is such a thing, they usually identify it with their personal pet project, pet peeve, or pet specialty, But Heerema knows it, and that is an utterly deadly knowledge to us. If he spreads this infection to your patient, all is lost.

The center, of course, is the one so well known and enacted by that frightening woman whose very name hurts us more than any other except the Enemy's Son Himself, the woman who said simply, "Be it done unto me according to your word." There are many names for it: the life of sanctity, willing the Enemy's will, loving the Enemy with one's whole heart and soul and mind and strength—of course that's the heart and center of it all, and there's absolutely no excuse for any of them not to know this. It's no esoteric secret. It's in every book in their Bible and said by every one of the saints. But a divided mind and heart have great difficulty seeing the simple, undivided center; they tend to project their own inner divisions out onto the data, the dogma.

Unfortunately, we've been quite unsuccessful in dividing and confusing Heerema's mind. He's rock-solid sure that there's just "one thing needful", and he knows exactly what it is. We've not been able to distract him into identifying sanctity with activism, as we have with most Americans.

(Quietism was the old heresy, activism is the new; they always come in pairs of opposites, so we can swing on them like a pendulum.)

He also knows that sanctity means contemplative prayer, is the point of the Bible, and requires fidelity to the Church. These are three things they used to know well, and even took for granted (e.g., in the Middle Ages), but most modern Christians no longer see this. The popular scholarly "wisdom" is now to contrast the biblical with the contemplative (which they claim is Greek), and to contrast the inner, personal life of sanctity with fidelity to the visible Church and her dogmas.

But Father Heerema hasn't fallen for this. He understands how contemplative the Bible is, and he understands hundreds of passages that no noncontemplative understands, from his own experience. He also understands that the whole purpose of the Church and of everything in it, from fund-raising to encyclicals, from papal plane rides to printing presses, is to spread the infection of sanctity.

He teaches theology; simply theology. Specialization has divided their theology into competing compartments: dogmatic, moral, sacramental, ecclesiastical, Christological, apologetic and social, to name a few. But this man roots every one of these fields in this center that he knows so well and relates this center to all the fields. He knows the theological hub of the wheel where all the spokes meet, and this transforms each of the spokes, the separate fields, as follows. (See how he has avoided our standard traps.)

Most dogmatic theologians are intellectuals, more like philosophers than saints. But not Heerema. Let me give you one example. He solves the hermeneutical problem, the problem of interpretation, which has vexed, pre-occupied and distracted hundreds of theologians for thousands of hours, as simply as the Enemy's Son did when He said to the unbelievers, "If your will were to do the will of my Father, you would understand my doctrine." What scandalous simplicity!

In moral theology, most theologians today are minimalists, trying to get away with something—some compromise, some weakening and watering down. But Heerema not only teaches them to go the extra mile for the Enemy but he knows and extols the joy that comes from it. He even dares to talk about the joy of sacrifice and the joy of suffering. It's old, unoriginal stuff, of course, but most of them have long abandoned it.

In sacramental theology, instead of getting tangled in any of the possible peripheral distractions, he emphasizes Communion as personal love and intimacy with the Enemy's Son. See the picture?

In ecclesiology, instead of picking up the sword in the current controversies about Church authority, he simply radiates gratitude to the Church as his mother. He doesn't just defend her, he loves her. Most students have never seen this phenomenon before.

In Christology, he has, of course, a traditional, "high" view; but it's obvious that it's been lived as well as thought. He talks about the Enemy's Son as if He were his best friend—because He is. And he invites his students to get to know Him too, not just to know *about* Him.

In apologetics, it's clear that he's not only out to win arguments, but to win souls. His simple honesty does more harm than subtler intellects, but most terrifying of all is his love. His apologetics is missionary work for his Beloved.

Even when he gets into social, political and economic issues, he sees a relationship between them and that center. For instance, he's suspicious of the economics of both the right (unrestricted capitalism) and the left (state socialism) because he sees the effects both these systems tend to have on souls: the materialism, the greed, the envy. He doesn't defend or ignore right-wing death squads or left-wing terror; he just fights for life. (By the way, he was also in jail for Operation Rescue. He won over more students from his jail cell than he did from his classroom.)

He also relates his theology to other subjects, in the way Newman wanted them to, but few of them ever do. In most Catholic schools today we can contemplate the living comedy of a total incomprehension about what a Catholic school means, both subjectively and objectively: On the one hand, there is rarely that personal sanctity that enlightens every subject, and on the other hand, no one quite knows how theology can integrate all other subjects any more. No one calls it "the Queen of the Sciences", as they all did in the Middle Ages. They let every other subject dictate to and determine theology, but they don't let theology dictate to or determine other subjects. Heerema reverses that.

He also integrates theory and practice. He's constantly connecting abstract theological dogmas like the hypostatic union with concrete choices his students make, like whether to have sex tonight. Of course, we see the connection clearly, but most mortals don't: If they deny the full divinity and humanity of the Enemy's Son, He loses His total authority over their lives—just what their strongest desires are waiting for!

Heerema even connects sexual fidelity with the old unpopular idea of the liberal arts, the love of truth for its own sake. In the lecture your patient sat in on, he explained that if you treat people as means to the end of sexual pleasure, you get into the habit of treating ideas also as means to some personal, practical end, whether pleasure (amusement), power (fame), or honor (acceptance, fashionability), rather than respecting the truth for its own sake. He got them to see the connection between purity of mind and purity of body.

So you see what a dangerous character he is. Few of them talk like that. Most of them don't talk either about the old dogmas or about real life, but when they do, they rarely connect them. But Heerema connects the Enemy's Son with everything, especially the things that are the students' real life concerns: sex, friendship, suicide, parents, alcohol, divorce, fear, pressures, drugs, rock music, marriage, money and depression. He so connects the Enemy's Son with everything that it's almost like turning the clock back 2,000 years and hearing Him talk again. Heerema actually takes seriously that verse about taking every thought captive and giving it to Him. We haven't been able to get him to worship at the great American shrine of Freedom of Thought. He positively loves to bow.

I don't know whether it's fortunate or not that his intellect is mediocre. Of course, if he were brilliant, we might have another Augustine or Aquinas to worry about. But the fact that he's so ordinary means that students can identify with him and easily aspire to be like him, no matter how ordinary they are. That's the danger for your patient now.

You let him see something new in that classroom: the fire within, the flame that sprung up in his heart when the flint of life and the steel of dogma met and sparked. We've never been able to dim that light. That's how we lost the whole world once to twelve ordinary men. Not all the novelties of Avant Garde or the rhetoric of Father Fenster can rival that light.

Do something about it, Braintwister. Immediately. You know how Our Father Below hates to lose. But I'm sure you'll have ample opportunity to explain your failure to Infernal Affairs.

Your increasingly ravenous uncle,

Snakebite

APPENDIX

"RETHINKING 199–: A REVISIONIST VIEW" A RESPONSE TO THE ANNUAL REPORT, NORTH AMERICAN DIVISION (NAD)

Comments by the Honorable E. Wormwood Snakebite
Deputy Director, Strategic Planning
and Analysis, Central Command
Director, Special Task Force on
Staff Productivity, Central Command

Delivered to Divisional HQ Personnel,
Section Chiefs and Senior Case Officers
15 January 199–. Restricted.

My dear colleagues,

First, I want to thank the NAD executive team for the warmth and authentic good will they always show me at these annual sessions. May your faithful service to the will of Our Father Below keep you always from the unfortunate (I can assure you) state of those who disappoint his expectations. A bit of sage advice to you younger devils: Do look behind you now and then!

(Laughter.)

I have just read—as I'm sure you all have—your latest year-end report, with attached audit from the Department of

Infernal Revenue. On the surface, this year's statistics must provoke in any spiritually mature fiend a certain satisfaction, a sense of genuine achievement: American moral indices are not merely down, but in a virtual crash-dive.

Surely we can consider 199– a banner year: Murders and abortions up; rape, sodomy, consumer debt, domestic violence, chemical dependency, divorce, suicide, liposuctions, television sales, plastic surgeries and homelessness all on the upswing; poverty growing by the minute; the budget deficit, the erosion of the work ethic and the breakup of the family each moving briskly apace—truly, we can all be "bullish on America".

And these are not just haphazard developments, mind you. We've managed over the past 40 years or so to create some highly efficient industries to further our aims. And—a gratifying irony—we've cajoled record numbers of the human vermin into doing our work for us.

Perhaps never since the fall of the Roman Empire has it required so little effort to prosecute our Agenda as it does today. Doubtless, that's why so many of you have been observed away from your desks this year, whiling away the time at Our Father's abundant recreational facilities. (Suffice it to say, gentlemen, all derelictions of duty have been carefully noted.)

... Where was I? Oh yes. Getting our historic enemy, the human race, to do our work for us. In a century of remarkable progress, this continues to be our crowning achievement.

For example, in the past, we managed to ensnare individuals here and there in the—for them—delicious bonds of lust. The case of Casanova comes to mind, a triumph of my own humble efforts.

(Polite applause.)

Today, however, through the miracle of central planning, we've managed to develop an entire industry dedicated to getting people to view lust through our uniquely crafted rose-colored lenses (further evidence, I might add, of our continuing technological edge). Day by day, through advertising, radio, television, movies and music, generations are being formed to believe that sexual license is the way to personal liberation. Things have come to such a pass that one scarcely need tempt anyone anymore. Chastity is now so easy a target in some urban settings that veteran officers routinely delegate the work.

Hardly anyone in the human camp bothers to do even a few minimal calculations. To notice, for example, the connections between sexual license and rape, between lust and the divorce rate, between pornography and violence against women. Yes, I know, there were those in the Head Office who doubted the usefulness of the social sciences. But today, in all candor, even Our Father Below—himself once a skeptic—acknowledges that the dysfunctions we've inserted into human society would lack all intellectual credibility without them—properly managed, of course. As a result, our great task of deconstruction proceeds virtually unhindered. I'm sure you share my anticipation for Phase 2: escalating violence, seething resentment between the sexes, spousal murders by the thousands, child abuse and incest on a hitherto unimagined scale—it promises to be the most entertaining epoch since the Visigoths.

Those few human voices calling the Agenda into question are simply no match for our experts in the "helping professions"—a marvelous phrase—who assure people that sexual restraint is positively bad for one's health.

Little wonder that some of you have become, shall we say, a trifle lax in your efforts of late. (A word to the wise: The path to command positions is narrow and steep; many are called but few are chosen.)

The "death industry" is another one of our more recent triumphs. Oh, to be sure, abortion and infanticide were always with us. But, like lust, in the past they were largely confined to individuals. Today however, we've captured millions in the efficient drift-nets of our "quick fix" ethics. Ignorant of the enrichment which flows from facing the consequences of one's actions, happily unmindful of the Heavenly Enemy's mercies, they line up for our services like gas guzzlers in an oil shortage. How blissfully we play on their fears, robbing them all the while of the prophets and saints, the artists and beauties with which the Opposition planned to provide them.

And the lure of riches? Well, one scarcely knows how to tabulate recent gains.

The bane of a few aristocrats several centuries ago, we've managed, through an adroit gene-splicing of democracy, to infect nearly everyone today with the illusions of wealth. Even the poorest of the poor these days carry the virus of acquisitiveness, clutching in their loathsome little paws the tokens of our consumeroid paradise. Yes, brothers, we've created a whole culture built on the notion that human worth is measured by the car one drives or the labels attached to one's handbag.

We make sure that the fools spend so much time and energy acquiring their beloved trifles that they have little opportunity for—may Our Father preserve us—reflection. Most of them, luckily, die without a clue as to who they really are and how spiritually vapid their lives have become.

Well, with results like these under your belts, most of you are eager to roll up your adultery-cluster charts and head for the spa, yes?

Not so fast, my dear sprites.

America will hardly "go to Hell in a handbasket", appealing as that imagery may be, if professionals like you continue to take things for granted. Let me caution you as forcefully as I can: The trends are not nearly so positive as you imagine. (I'm saying this for your own good, of course, and purely as a concerned friend who argues your case at Head Office.)

As you all know, I have long moved in the lowest official circles of the lowerarchy. And in those official circles, your negligence toward the finer points of our great task has not gone unnoticed. In fact, it has sparked considerable disappointment from Our Father Himself.

I trust I have your attention? Good. Then listen well. First, contrary to conventional wisdom, the Head Office is not interested in mere numbers. Forget your pathetic statistical data on falling church attendance—that won't earn you any kudos Downstairs, I can assure you.

You will recall that in the Enemy's Detestable Book, Our Father Below is referred to as a serpent, "subtlest of all the creatures". A typical Enemy understatement that hardly captures the nuance, the real art, of Our Father's genius. Nonetheless, essentially true: Our Father has a particular taste for subtlety, gentlemen, not the dull-headed wickedness we see in your report, so crude, so obvious, so appropriate to a first-term plebe at the academy.

Need I remind you of your colleagues who presided over the recent catastrophe in Eastern Europe? They watched 70 years of relentless work evaporate overnight. All of them, from senior staff to field agents, are currently undergoing appropriate therapy.

Yes, I can see that you've heard their shrieks echoing upward from a variety of intimate rehabilitation sessions. They trusted in numbers, too: so many members of the party, so many nuclear warheads, so many prisoners in the gulag. Gentlemen, don't make their mistake.

And why, you ask, did our Soviet Studies program fail so completely? A lack of subtlety. If our triumphs are too vulgar, it only gives the Enemy Above opportunities for mischief. Clear evil attracts precious few souls, my dear friends. If we show our hand too coarsely, what happens? People stampede to the Enemy's camp. Subterfuge, that's the metier of Our Father Below.

That's why it's vital that we operate always, without exception, in disguise. If the fools can't see that what we're offering them is evil, our Agenda can reach so much farther and penetrate their miserable little personalities so much more deeply. They never know what's hit them until it's (hopefully) too late.

For example: Who would dispute that youth and health are good things? But if we can make humans a slave to these qualities, make them run from their mortality obsessively and deny death even though, of course, it is inescapable—then we have them!

And what about self-esteem? Now that's terribly important for humans, isn't it? But we all know that if the fools had the slightest inkling of the greatness planted by the Enemy within them, we might as well pack our bags and go home. Deflect that possibility by making self-esteem the highest of all values. (And never let them get a glimmer that it comes from their link with the Enemy!) Soon we'll have them isolated, unable to trust, incapable of subordinating themselves to a higher cause or another's needs. You see, it's really quite simple. You can even let them pray, if you must.

Heresy, you say? Certainly not. While I admit the repugnance of the topic, there is promise even here. If your client starts on the path to prayer, just don't let him discover what prayer is for. Naturally, you need to involve our agents in the field, our experts in this area. Make sure that your human never gets the idea that prayer means real contact with the Enemy and His forces. Convince him that he's really getting in touch with his own deeper self. You know the approach: "the god within" plan. Then, I assure you, even so explosive a substance as prayer can be handled without fear.

Get the idea, gentlemen? Bang them over the head with naked displays of malice, and you leave their precious souls scarcely scathed. And believe me, we're in the business of scathing souls, in case you've forgotten. Our real work requires a delicate touch, a soothing voice, a friendly demeanor, poison flavored with kindness. I want snakes in the grass, not accountants.

In the end, we must always remember the Ultimate Plan of the Master whose purposes we serve. I, for one, shall never forget that day when the Enemy Above announced His absurd scheme not only to create the human vermin but—it wounds me even to say the words—to elevate these beasts above us angelic beings, and—worse still—to decree that we should serve them.

Our Father Below rightly protested this lunacy before the Throne itself as an unconscionable insult to the angelic host—we, creation's firstborn.

But when the Enemy countered that His "love" for the little swine was such that He planned to empty Himself of His awesome dignity to become—the idea appalls me—one of them, we knew then that it was war, a struggle to the finish—war against the Enemy's deluded scheme and war against the human race, His wretched darlings.

In prosecuting our cause, always remember the motto of Our Father Below: "The defeat of the human vermin is the triumph of right order, common sense and angelic dignity." How urgently, how passionately, we must take this wisdom to heart as 199– stretches before us, rich in its opportunities!

So, let us labor with a hunger that befits our standing, my dear friends. And no more lollygagging around the rec rooms or—if you'll pardon the irreverence—there'll be Hell to pay.

ACKNOWLEDGMENT

Special thanks to Gabriel Meyer for his extensive help with Snakebite's "Rethinking 199-: A Revisionist View", and to Francis X. Maier for his editing and creative input.